# Poetry and What Is Real

*Richard Tillinghast*

# Poetry and
# What Is Real

To Rory,
hoping you
will enjoy these —

Richard
Tillinghast
July 2009

**THE UNIVERSITY OF MICHIGAN PRESS**

*Ann Arbor*

*This book is dedicated to Alan Williamson,*
*remembering conversations on poetry*
*that have continued for over forty years,*
*in Cambridge, Berkeley and elsewhere*

Copyright © by the University of Michigan 2004
All rights reserved
Published in the United States of America by
The University of Michigan Press
Manufactured in the United States of America
∞ Printed on acid-free paper

2007   2006   2005   2004      4   3   2   1

*A CIP catalog record for this book is available from the British Library.*

Library of Congress Cataloging-in-Publication Data

Tillinghast, Richard.
    Poetry and what is real / Richard Tillinghast.
        p.   cm. — (Poets on poetry)
    ISBN 0-472-09872-1 (alk. paper) — ISBN 0-472-06872-5 (pbk. :
alk. paper)
        1. American poetry—20th century—History and criticism.   2.
Poetry—Authorship.   3. Poetry.   I. Title.   II. Series.
    PS323.5.T55   2004
    811'.509—dc22                                      2004004959

# Preface

Things that can never be sustainable and thus "real" in everyday life, fantasies of one kind or another, wishes that can never come true, are often the meat and drink of the poetry written by the authors I write about in this book: Allen Ginsberg, James Dickey, W. H. Auden, Elizabeth Bishop, Robert Lowell, Sylvia Plath, and others. Robert Frost writes in "Spring Pools":

> The trees that have it in their pent-up buds
> To darken nature and be summer woods—
> Let them think twice before they use their powers
> To blot out and drink up and sweep away
> These flowery waters and these watery flowers
> From snow that melted only yesterday.

No one expects the trees to "think twice," or even once; but the appeal Frost makes to them satisfies something in us, as it no doubt satisfied something in him. "I Was Born in Lucerne," begins a poem by Philip Levine. "Everyone says otherwise. They take me / to a flat on Pingree in Detroit / and say, up there, the second floor."

Moving from these inner struggles to the public realm, I believe that poetry can still, despite all that has been written about its marginalization in American culture, make a contribution to the common good. That contribution begins with the poet's refusal to accept the world as defined by received opinion. In "Seeing Things" Seamus Heaney asserts: "whatever is given // Can always be reimagined, however four-square, / Plank-thick, hull- stupid and out of its time / It happens to be." Heaney has used his poetry as a way of helping move contemporary Ireland toward a redefinition of its divided cultural heritage, toward reconciliation and an integration of the conflicting strands of its history. The current book restricts itself, with one or two exceptions, to a consideration of how poetry is practiced in the United States. But Ireland, as a parallel English-speaking literary culture, exists as a kind of shadow presence in my book, because it offers an example of how poetry might ideally function within our own culture if we could become less fixated on "celebrity" and popular entertainment. America is too young and too important in the world for us to give up on it just yet.

The title of this collection is from the title of an essay on Robert Lowell, whom I have written about more than about any other poet. If Heaney's career demonstrates the strength of poetry as a healing force within society, Lowell's poetry dramatizes an internal struggle for wholeness. For him "what is real" was both an ontological and a personal problem, because he often found himself in a state where he could not distinguish between fantasy and the phenomenological world. "The cat walks out—" he wrote during one of his manic phases, "or does it?" He continues, addressing his wife: "You can't be here, and yet we try to talk; / Somebody else is farcing in your face . . ." In connection with Lowell my title implies a different and extreme statement of the issue. Yet a subject I explore in "Quincy House and the White House" is that for all his personal turmoil, Lowell never gave up on poetry's responsibility to the *res publica*.

A poem is best read, at first anyway, on its own—with no need of biographical or historical background, no guide other than a dictionary. But throughout my life as a reader, I have consistently wanted to learn about the authors of my favorite books and poems. For me it would in fact be a very strange reader who did not want to know things about the authors of his or her favorite books. Many of my essays have a biographical dimension. One thing we all have in common is that each of us is living this mysterious thing called life, and we want to know how other people manage it—what their conflicts and compromises, failures and triumphs have been. Unlike Jacqueline Rose, the author of a book about Sylvia Plath that I examine in my Plath essay, who states, "This book starts from the assumption that Plath is a fantasy," the biographical parts of my essays make the attempt, even if the attempt is ultimately futile, to come as close as possible to getting the most accurate picture of my subjects.

Of all the poets I write about here, only Bob Dylan is an exact contemporary of mine. I have avoided writing about the poets of my own generation. This book presents, unsystematically, a small portrait gallery of poetic ancestors and guides. Though my emphasis is on American poets, I have included essays on a major English and a major Irish writer, Auden and Yeats. Since I count more than a few of these poets among those on whose example I formed my own taste in the art, this book is a retrospective of my life as a reader. It sketches a tradition within which I place my own poetry. While writing essays that I hope will illuminate the work and the lives of some of my favorite poets, I live a life in poetry myself, and I have woven into these pages some observations on the life, the craft, and the culture (or subculture) of poetry. "In Praise of Rhyme" and "Household Economy, Ruthlessness, Romance, and the Art of Hospitality: Notes on Revision" address technical aspects of the art. An autobiographical narrative I was asked to write for the Contemporary Authors series rounds out the book. Though I wrote it almost ten years ago, it seems complete enough in itself to keep me from wanting to revise it here.

Finally I come to the role of travel in my writing life. Experiencing other cultures firsthand helps the traveler see his or her own culture more clearly. At least I hope so. But travel is, above any other claim I would make for it, a form of intoxication. Thus it is intertwined with poetic inspiration, and often acts as such in my life as a writer. The exotic is a suspect category at this moment in our cultural history. But the word and the idea have been with us since the time of the ancient Greeks: *exotikos,* from *exo,* "outside." Thus "different," "not like us" except in essential human ways: these are areas I like to explore, particularly in an age when computer technology is redefining and shrinking our concepts of travel. When I "go to" a place on my computer desktop, when I "visit" someone's website, including my own (<http://www.personal.umich.edu./~rwtill>), I'm not really going anywhere; I'm still sitting in front of my computer. Real travel is something entirely different. The first time I visited—really visited—Yeats's tower, Thoor Ballylee in County Galway, I learned immeasurably about the difference between the tower

Yeats lived in and the tower he made a symbol in his poetry. This told me a lot about the inner and outer worlds of both Yeats and myself.

In *The Living House: An Anthropology of Architecture in South-East Asia,* Roxana Waterson makes the following observations: "'Tradition' . . . describes a process of handing down, and as such is just as dynamic and historical as any other social process. . . . Tradition, like history, is something that is continually being recreated and remodelled in the present . . ." I hope that *Poetry and What Is Real* will become for some readers a book that embodies a living tradition—how what we learn from the past becomes transformed in the present and transmitted to the future.

## Acknowledgments

*Poetry and What Is Real* represents the distillation of a quarter-century of my work as an essayist and literary journalist. In citing the publication history of these pieces, I would like to acknowledge the extremely pleasant and productive relationships I have had with a number of editors, some of whom I have known primarily through correspondence, fax and email, and through telephone conversations where interpretations, sentences and paragraphs have been weighed and debated.

Earlier versions of these essays have appeared in a number of periodicals. "Allen Ginsberg and His Generation" combines a piece by the same name that appeared in the *Boston Review* with one called "Birdbrain!" from an issue of *Parnassus* edited by Bill Harmon. "Donald Hall: Top of the 11th, Top of the Order" and "W. B. Yeats: The Labyrinth of Another's Being" first came out in the *New Criterion,* whose editors Hilton Kramer and Roger Kimball have been consistently encouraging and supportive of my endeavors as an essayist. I was particularly pleased with their enthusiasm for my essay on John Crowe Ransom—hardly a fashionable poet in 1997, when the essay appeared, or even now. The *New Criterion* has welcomed almost every proposal I have made to them for new work—though Hilton Kramer once rejected a Irish piece he had assigned me to write on the grounds that my view of Irish history was "somewhat to the left of the IRA."

"James Dickey: The Whole Motion" first saw the light of day in the *Southern Review* under the editorship of Dave Smith. "The Life and Fables of Bob Dylan" reworks an article from an issue of the *Missouri Review* where poets were asked to write about musicians, in combination with a longer piece called "Nothing Is Revealed: The Life and Significance of Bob Dylan" from the *Michigan Quarterly Review,* whose editor, Larry Goldstein, has been a longtime friend and colleague. I wrote the Elizabeth Bishop piece, "'How Different I Am from What They Think,'" and "Philip Levine: Working the Night Shift" for the *New York Times Book Review;* D. J. R. Bruckner, my editor there, I know only as a dry, sardonic voice on the phone. "W. H. Auden: 'Stop All the Clocks'" and "Digging for the Truth about Sylvia Plath" were published in the *Gettysburg Review,* where they benefited from the exacting editorial eye of Peter Stitt. "Blueberries Sprinkled with Salt: Frost's Letters" was written for the *Sewanee Review* when the late Andrew Lytle was its editor. As a senior at Sewanee I was Mr. Lytle's editorial assistant, and I think my year in that office gave me my sense of what a literary magazine should be. "Louis Simpson: The Poet of the 5:51" was written for the *Nation.*

"In Praise of Rhyme" was written for the twentieth anniversary of *Ploughshares,* another journal I have been closely associated with since its early days of publication. I was asked to write about a subject of my own choosing, and I find few people writing about rhyme these days. When Chase Twichell and Robin Behn were assembling their indispensable book, *The Practice of Poetry,* they asked me for a contribution, and it was enjoyable to address the subject of revision. Both the Robert Lowell essays were published in the *Kenyon Review,* which felt right to me, since Kenyon College was so important in Lowell's development as a young poet. Thanks to *Kenyon*'s editor, David Lynn, for his interest in these pieces. They are rather different: "Quincy House and the White House" addresses the public stances Lowell took at the height of his career; "Early and Late" is about Lowell's style and how it changed from his early days as a poet into his maturity. Maire Mhac an tSaoi was kind enough to publish "Travel and the Sense of Place" in *Poetry Ireland Review* during the year my family and I lived in Ireland in the early 1990s.

# Contents

# Allen Ginsberg and His Generation

The two poems for which Allen Ginsberg will be remembered were written almost fifty years ago. I'm speaking, of course, of "Kaddish" and "Howl." This makes the last five or six hundred pages of his *Collected Poems* pretty tough sledding. In terms of staying power, the Beats—Ginsberg, Ferlinghetti, Kerouac, Corso, et al.—flashed and faded. A line from Robert Lowell's "Waking in the Blue" serves as commentary: "These victorious figures of bravado ossified young."

Yet if there is one truth to be gleaned from surveying poetic careers, it is that no one can be sure of his or her ability to keep writing at any achieved level of intensity. In *Poetry and the Age* Randall Jarrell puts it well:

> A man who is a good poet at forty may turn out to be a good poet at sixty; but he is more likely to have stopped writing poems, to be doing exercises in his own manner, or to have reverted to whatever commonplaces were popular when he was young. A good poet is someone who manages, in a lifetime of standing out in thunderstorms, to be struck by lightning five or six times; a dozen or two dozen times and he is great.

Jarrell was writing about Wallace Stevens's *Auroras of Autumn,* but his remarks apply to what happened to Allen Ginsberg.

Ginsberg broke into print in 1956 as a poet of undeniable power. "Howl" was just what the name implied: a cry of loneli-

---

Review of *Allen Ginsberg, Collected Poems: 1947–1980* (New York: Harper and Row, 1984) and *On the Poetry of Allen Ginsberg,* ed. Lewis Hyde (Ann Arbor: University of Michigan Press, 1984). Earlier versions appeared in the *Boston Review* and *Parnassus.*

ness and longing—late-night, animalistic, piercing. Inspired by Whitman's spirit and line, it is a poem that Walt himself would have been proud to have penned. Ginsberg's imaginative fecundity "birthed" his long, dazzling, breath-launched lines, and his wild manipulations of rhetorical logic are as exhilarating today as they were half a century ago. It was Ginsberg who invented the unexpected adjective-noun combination—"negro streets," "pubic beards," "stale beer afternoon"—that later became Bob Dylan's trademark: "neon madmen," "honky-tonk lagoon," "jingle-jangle morning." He also coined a certain type of disjunctive noun-with-prepositional-phrase formula: "machinery of night," "scholars of war," "Peyote solidities of halls." These constructions did more than create atmosphere. They were Ginsberg's way of reprogramming the language to make it suggest in shorthand some of his favorite ideas: that America was racist, corrupt, and dangerous; that addiction characterized not merely a fringe, but society as a whole; that madness and deviance were, in this frightening, monolithic society, somehow "holy" (also a favorite word of Blake's). A decade or two later these ideas became so widely accepted as to be commonplace.

Besides giving voice to the experience of a generation—one that would become surprisingly influential—"Howl" is at once tragic and very, very funny. The magic is in the voice. The momentum of rhetoric becomes so powerful in the poem that Ginsberg can throw in asides that comment on the action while still not breaking the headlong rush of language:

> who jumped off the Brooklyn Bridge this actually
> happened and walked away unknown and forgotten into
> the ghostly daze of Chinatown soup alleyways &
> firetrucks, not even one free beer . . .

As the 1950s belatedly became the notorious '60s, Ginsberg the poet, outraged and outrageous, became Ginsberg the hippie court-jester and publicist for worthy causes. While his poetic example may have been responsible for the appearance of a certain amount of flatulence and apocalyptic soapbox raving in our poetry, his hot air helped thaw the frozen '50s. He showed writers as different from himself as Robert Lowell how to use the colloquial American idiom and to speak more directly to their readers. He helped create a wider audience for poetry, which was, and is, still struggling to recover the readership it lost during the Modernist revolution.

But though the bearded, beaded, mantra-chanting poet is part of everyone's image of the 1960s "love generation," Ginsberg was always more of an old-fashioned earnest beatnik than a hippie. The celebratory tone of much of the '60s ran counter to his introspective, often morbid temperament, and his most characteristic poems express sadness, loss, and anger. His best work still carries the aura of beatnik days in North Beach, San Francisco: jazz and paranoia, black turtlenecks and Dago Red, coldwater flats and the Cold War, reefer madness, the Coexistence Bagel Shop, and speed-raps at the Café Trieste.

Although his public reading style went a long way toward covering up the absence of real quality in most of his later poetry, there is no doubt that Ginsberg did his best work early. Perhaps he was simply a poet of his time. Perhaps the fulfillment of his desire to have his vision validated through public recognition took the edge off his hunger. Perhaps his theory of composition, which he described as "First Thought, Best Thought," is a procedure better suited to Zen ink-drawing than to poetry.

Ginsberg was at one time a great stylist, and the artistic life of a writer who depends so heavily on style is precarious; in this regard Ginsberg's decline, oddly, resembles Hemingway's. Over the years Ginsberg's style coarsened, he lost his inventiveness and became bombastic. The main things that disappeared were his playfulness, his wit, and his quickness. Here is a passage from "Howl" (1959):

I'm with you in Rockland
    where we wake up electrified out of the coma by our own
    souls' airplanes roaring over the roof they've come to
    drop angelic bombs the hospital illuminates itself
    imaginary walls collapse O skinny legions run outside
    O starry-spangled shock of mercy the eternal war is here
    O victory forget your underwear we're free

Now listen to this from "Birdbrain" (1980):

3

Birdbrain runs the World!
Birdbrain is the ultimate product of Capitalism
Birdbrain chief bureaucrat of Russia, yawning
Birdbrain ran FBI 30 years appointed by F. D. Roosevelt
   and never chased Cosa Nostra!
Birdbrain apportions wheat to he burned, keeps prices up
   on the world market!
Birdbrain lends money to Developing Nation police-states
   thru the International Monetary Fund!
Birdbrain never gets laid on his own he depends on his
   office to pimp for him
Birdbrain offers brain transplants in Switzerland
Birdbrain wakes up in middle of night and arranges his
   sheets
I am Birdbrain!

What happened to the poet who wrote "Howl"? Several things.
First, his old sense of compassion—which made a statement like
"I'm with you in Rockland" absolutely convincing— vanished
somewhere along the line. This is all the more ironic since he
had come to think of himself as a Buddhist. There's no compassion in "Birdbrain"; it's all contempt. Another difference between "Howl" and "Birdbrain" is that there are real people bursting with contradictions in "Howl," people who "fell out of the
subway window, jumped in the filthy Passaic, leaped on negroes,
cried all over the street," and in other ways lived amid the dirt
and corruption of our society—and this makes the early Ginsberg's social pronouncements human and believable. The political statements in "Birdbrain!" on the other hand, are stale,
humorless, self-righteous. I like moments where poetry and journalism meet—Whitman does it all the time—but here, when
journalism comes in the front door, poetry ducks out the back.
   It's as though Ginsberg stopped listening to himself; he just
kept droning on out of habit. When finally he comes out and
says "I am Birdbrain!" one is inclined to respond: Yes, you are
Birdbrain, because you have stopped thinking. And whatever
happened to Ginsberg's wonderful sense of humor and timing,
which led him to toss "this actually happened" and "not even
one free beer" into the Niagara of his rhetoric, and to juggle levels of diction—the operatic and the intimate—in phrases like

"O victory forget your underwear we're free"? Some sort of deadening of feeling also seems to have taken place. "Howl" and "Kaddish" are as moving as they are because of the intense suffering that pervades them.

The decline of Allen Ginsberg's creative energies has parallels in other poets of his generation. A number of these poets did their best work soon after breaking away from formal verse. Perhaps the transition from the rigid to the free released energies previously held in check, while the memory of discipline infused the new, freer work with a sense of form. But while they apparently got a breath of fresh air from the increased sense of contact with their audience that accompanied the Vietnam War protest readings and from the sense of aliveness we all felt in those years, their subsequent work has suffered—perhaps from too easy acceptance, from a prevailing contempt for thought, and from a feeling that language itself is an inadequate tool of communication. Whatever the reason, these poets' later work is marked by an unearned facility with the language. Significantly, this generation of poets has lacked the kind of critical conscience that Randall Jarrell gave the poets (Robert Lowell, John Berryman, Delmore Schwartz) of the previous decade. Robert Bly was the dominant critic of the group that included James Wright, Donald Hall, and Galway Kinnell. His most notable contributions since the 1960s have concerned themselves with society, politics, psychology, myth, translation, and other subjects that, while they may help to broaden the poet's outlook, give writers little guidance in trying to discover the full resources of poetic language.

What conclusions can be drawn about the group of highly gifted poets who were born in the extraordinarily fecund late 1920s? All of them, except perhaps Robert Creeley, attempted to overcome the alienation from society that has been, since Rimbaud, both myth and powerful reality for poets. While they indeed found (and to some extent created) a wider audience and made their work "relevant" and even socially effective, they did so at some cost to their art. The ideal of a poetry that is valuable both as art and as social statement, with a few exceptions in particular poems, eluded them. Though the inspiring and catastrophic events and the wave of new ideas that we habitually refer to as the "The Sixties" are well behind us chronologically, these writers, like many other people who came of age in those years, are still at sea.

Good reading to supplement the *Collected Poems* can be found in *On the Poetry of Allen Ginsberg*, edited by Lewis Hyde, a rich treasury of prose commentary by and about Ginsberg. It's a chronicle of the times, and changing attitudes toward Ginsberg tell a story in themselves. Diana Trilling might not be much of a literary critic, but she gets high marks as a hygienist in "The Other Night at Columbia: A Report from the Academy," which describes a reading Ginsberg, Peter Orlovsky, and Gregory Corso gave at Columbia in 1958 or 1959:

> For me, it was of some note that the auditorium smelled fresh. The place was already full when we arrived; I took one look at the crowd and was certain that it would smell bad. But I was mistaken. These people may think they're dirty inside and dress up to it. But the audience was clean and Ginsberg was clean and Corso was clean and Orlovsky was clean. Maybe Ginsberg says he doesn't bathe or shave; Corso, I know, declares that he has never combed his hair; Orlovsky has a line in one of the two poems he read—he's not yet written his third, the chairman explained—"If I should shave, I know the bugs would go away." But for this occasion, at any rate, Ginsberg, Corso, and Orlovsky were all beautifully clean and shaven.

Isn't that reassuring? Mrs. Trilling was also concerned that Ginsberg "was appearing on the same Columbia platform from which T. S. Eliot had last year read his poetry; he was being presented by, and was thus bound to be thought under the sponsorship of, a distinguished member of the academic and literary community who was also one's long-time friend." Such was the hauteur of the academic elite half a century ago.

John Hollander, also in *Partisan Review,* wrote of this "very short and very tiresome book": "It is only fair to Allen Ginsberg . . . to remark on the utter lack of decorum of any kind in his dreadful little volume." Once Ginsberg had come to occupy the Walt Whitman Honorary Chair as America's Good Gray Poet, Mr. Hollander added this afterthought in 1984:

This review was written in my youth and in a sort of worked-up high dudgeon which echoed the high-camp-prophetic mode of *Howl*'s front matter, and which may have masked some of my disappointment in a turn I saw an old friend and poetic mentor to have taken. I only regret now that I hadn't given "America" and "In a Supermarket in California" time to register; I should have certainly commended them.

So, from author of a "dreadful little volume" to "old friend and poetic mentor": this sort of crow-eating from one of America's eminent academicians must have been delicious to Ginsberg.

Though attacked by Hollander, Norman Podhoretz, M. L. Rosenthal, *Time* magazine, James Dickey, and almost everyone else in the literary Establishment, Ginsberg had some stout defenders: Richard Eberhart, Allen Grossman, Harvey Shapiro, Louis Simpson, and Kenneth Rexroth among them. Then a point arrived where academia accepted Ginsberg as a kind of gay poet-saint. This must have happened around 1970, when adherents of the political counterculture and young academics discovered how much they had in common. They—we—were, after all, in many cases the same people. Yet by this time Ginsberg was essentially finished as a poet. In the *New York Times Book Review* in 1973 Helen Vendler wrote an astute assessment: "Concentration and exactness of focus are, when he is able to summon them, among Ginsberg's undeniable powers . . . The trouble with the present book [*Mind Breaths*] is that the minute particulars of mankind seem to be vanishing from Ginsberg's latest verse in favor of the minute particulars of geography." She also points correctly to a conceptual basis for the decline of human emotion and detailed sensory evocation: "a theory of poetry intending to 'include more simultaneous perceptions and relate previously unrelated (what were thought irrelevant) occurrences.'" I agree with her also on the point that Ginsberg's enthusiasm for Eastern religions translates poorly into English: "It is one thing to end an English poem with 'Shantih, shantih, shantih,' but to end 'Om Om Om Sa Ra Wa Bu Da Da Ki Ni Yea,' and so on for three more lines is disaster." What Vendler does not mention is that by the time of *Mind Breaths* Ginsberg had apparently become such a believer in the power of mantra that he felt it more important to release this power into the world than to write a good poem.

Timothy Leary's *Esquire* article "In the Beginning, Leary Turned on Ginsberg and Saw That It Was Good" makes fascinating reading and also gives an insight into Ginsberg's most basic obsessions. Here are Ginsberg and Orlovsky on acid:

> Allen picked up the white telephone and dialed Operator. The two thin figures leaned forward wrapped up in a holy fervor trying to spread peace. The dear noble innocent helplessness of the naked body. They looked as though they had stepped out of a *quattrocento* canvas, apostles, martyrs, dear fanatic holy men. Allen said, Hello, operator, this is God. I want to talk to Kerouac. To whom do I want to talk? Kerouac. What's my name? This is God. G-O-D. Okay. We'll try Capitol 7-0563. Where? Northport, Long Island. There was a pause. We were all listening hard. Oh. Yes. That's right. That's the number of the house where I was born.

Comments on Ginsberg from a gay perspective are of more than passing interest, since this peer group has some insights that are not available to the population at large. Charley Shively of *Gay Sunshine* discusses Ginsberg's particular brand of homosexuality:

> What are we to say about our mad, divine impassioned loves for these superstud he-men such as Neal and Jack? . . . Herbert Huncke and William Burroughs, bold and clear homosexuals who were also early companions of Ginsberg . . . have never inspired the intimate love, devotion, ecstasy and poetry of Cassady or Kerouac's images (even in decay and ashes) . . . Why is it that the stud image can bring us faggots sooner to poetry and tears than few other things?

Shively questions Ginsberg's macho gayness and identifies him as a misogynist: "Much of the butch disrespect for women in Cassady and Kerouac has rubbed off onto Ginsberg. (We'll pass over the unkind things he says about 'closet queens' and 'teacup faggots.') In Ginsberg's poetry and conversation, women are always called 'girls' and their names are seldom used." His homosexuality would seem to come out of the old-fashioned American "queer" scene of locker rooms, jails, Ys, and railroad yards—in other words, the scene introduced to Ginsberg by his two bisexual muses, Kerouac and Cassady.

To return to the poems themselves. Much of the apprentice work that preceded "Howl" sounds like the magazine verse of the 1950s. Here is "Ode: My 24th Year":

> Now I have become a man
> and know no more than mankind can
> and groan with nature's every groan,
> transcending child's blind skeleton
> and all childish divinity,
> while loomed in consanguinity
> the weaving of the shroud goes on.

But the transition from this immature work to Ginsberg at the height of his powers was not abrupt. *The Green Automobile,* a transitional volume, shows glimmers of the highly emotional and the visionary mix that characterizes the mature work:

> The windshield's full of tears,
>         rain wets our naked breasts,
>     we kneel together in the shade
>             amid the traffic of night in paradise.

When Ginsberg finally did become the masterly and inspired poet who wrote "Howl," he had evolved a style capable of expressing his vision—apocalyptic, despairing, visionary, homoerotic, political—by means of bold, simple rhetorical devices. The first of these devices is anaphora, the employment of lines and phrases beginning with the same word. In the liner notes to *Allen Ginsberg Reads Howl and Other Poems* he writes: "I depended on the word 'who' to keep the beat, a base to keep measure, return to and take off again onto another streak of invention." In the use of anaphora Ginsberg owes something to Whitman and to Christopher Smart. But ancient Hebrew prosody is the ultimate source of this device, which is strikingly appropriate to Ginsberg's role as prophet-poet—the marriage of poet and prosody here seems almost atavistic. After all, Smart's "Jubilate

Agno" is a half-parodic, half-serious pastiche of the Psalms, and Whitman is said to have been influenced by the Biblical cadences of the Quaker preachers he heard as a boy.

The Fall of Ginsberg evidenced itself stylistically in two different directions: a loss of verbal energy and an opposite tendency to hype the language with willed, unconvincing rhetoric. Both tendencies can be seen as early as the middle '60s in a poem that has been called one of Ginsberg's best, "Wichita Vortex Sutra." I went to sleep twice last night trying to reread the poem. Here's an example from "Wichita" of Ginsberg's lax, nothing-happening use of language (did I read somewhere that he dictated this poem into a tape recorder?):

> Approaching Salina,
> Prehistoric excavation, *Apache Uprising*
> in the drive-in theater
> > Shelling Bombing Range mapped in the distance,
> > Crime Prevention Show, sponsor Wrigley's Spearmint
> > Dinosaur Sinclair advertisement, glowing green—
> South 9th Street lined with poplar & elm branch
> > > spread over evening's tiny headlights—
> > Salina Highschool's brick darkens Gothic
> over a night-lit door—

This is nothing but shorthand, the dead end of Pound's insistence on poetic compression and the omission of articles. Note the lack of verbs, and especially the poverty of syntax. By contrast "Howl" is written, and is full of complex sentences. The content here is travel notes—"particulars of geography," as Vendler puts it.

An example of Ginsberg's increasingly hollow-sounding rhetoric, with its de rigueur exclamations and apostrophes and archaic usages, from the same poem:

> Kansas! Kansas! Shuddering at last!
> > PERSON appearing in Kansas!
> angry telephone calls to the University
> Police dumbfounded leaning on
> > > their radiocar hoods
> While Poets chant to Allah in the roadhouse Showboat!

Blue eyed children dance and hold thy Hand O aged Walt
who came from Lawrence to Topeka to envision
Iron interlaced upon the city plain—
Telegraph wires strung from city to city O Melville!

I could go on. But why beat a dead fish? This passage has the flimsiness of journalism without even journalism's attention to facts to rescue it from its bathetic wallowing. Ginsberg performed a valuable role as social critic and gadfly, culture hero of the '60s, but really he was finished as a poet very early on, another of the "best minds of my generation"—destroyed in his case, not by madness, but by fame, self-imitation, and complacency.

But how much smaller and duller contemporary American poetry would have been without Allen Ginsberg! Is there a living poet who can claim not to have been influenced by Ginsberg's openness and exuberance? He was, in addition, a leading actor in the liberation movements associated with the '60s and '70s. In fact, it may have been his activities as prophetic bard and social critic that drained energy from his poetry. His decline is a disappointment, but his achievement is real and lasting. The wit and charm of lines like these from "America" (1956) are as fresh now as they were when they were first written:

America this is quite serious.
America this is the impression I get from looking in the
    television set.
America is this correct?
I'd better get right down to the job.
It's true I don't want to join the Army or turn lathes in
    precision parts factories, I'm nearsighted and
    psychopathic anyway.
America I'm putting my queer shoulder to the wheel.

# Donald Hall

## *Top of the 11th, Top of the Order*

"The task and potential greatness of mortals," in the words of Hannah Arendt as quoted by Donald Hall at the beginning of his eleventh book of poems, *The Museum of Clear Ideas,* "reside in their ability to produce things which are at home in everlastingness." In this collection, Hall's strategy for being "at home in everlastingness" organizes itself around three emphases: a seven-page elegy for a fictitious poet of our time called Bill Trout; a long, nine-part poem called "Baseball," the sections of which are innings, written in nine-syllable lines; and the long title sequence, an omnium gatherum modeled after Horace's odes. There is in addition a reprise called "Extra Innings."

Being a particularly trusting reader, the first time I read "Another Elegy" I missed Hall's broad hint, delivered in the form of an epigraph from T. S. Eliot: "Both one and many; in the brown baked features / The eyes of a familiar compound ghost . . ." But I'm glad I was credulous enough to read the poem at least once under the impression that Bill Trout was a real person—or at least wondering which real-life poet Hall had in mind when he was imagining the character.

My credulity was not badly misplaced, because in Bill Trout, Hall has sketched a composite picture of his generation of poets. In the pastiche of a biographical sketch from *The Norton Anthology of Contemporary Verse* that Hall has appended in his notes to the book, Trout's dates are 1927–77: born in the same year as John Ashbery, Galway Kinnell, W. S. Merwin, and James

---

Review of *The Museum of Clear Ideas* (New York: Ticknor and Fields, 1993). From the *New Criterion.*

Wright; one year later than A. R. Ammons, Robert Creeley, Allen Ginsberg, and Frank O'Hara; and a year before Philip Levine and Donald Hall. Trout is a poet from the heartland: "Idaho made him," Hall writes, tongue gleefully in cheek, "Pocatello of hobos and freightyards— / clangor of iron, fetor of coalsmoke." His literary beginnings are those of the home-grown American verse-maker: "When he was fifteen he stayed home from fishing to number / feet that promenaded to a Union Pacific tune, ABAB / pentameters."

His excesses and troubles are those of mid-century American poets like Lowell, Schwartz, and Berryman: madness, divorce, and alcoholism. As the parody blurb puts it, "Trout led a troubled life, more like the generation of his teachers than his own generation." The genius of the fictional portrait lies in the familiarity of the generic story: "he drank two Guggenheims and snorted / an NEA." Hall deftly sketches scenes that give the story its verisimilitude. The tone and the vocabulary epitomize the period. At a reunion of old friends in the 1960s, Bill, recently divorced, "paced / muttering, smoking his Lucky Strikes. Later the rest / divorced and paced."

Typically, it is on the quintessentially American occasion of families gathering for a camping and fishing trip—"setting up tents, joking, frying pickerel in cool dusk"—that Trout must spoil the idyll with his bathetic animadversions on existence: "Continually sloshed, Bill proclaimed / that life was shit, death was shit—even shit was shit." Hall does not answer the often-posed question of why the writers of our time—particularly the poets—have led lives of excess, breakdown, and despair. Finally, though, amidst the wreckage and dreck of the generic poet's life, Hall celebrates and marvels at the irreducible calculus of hard work and dedication of a writer's life:

> Bill Trout
> woke up, the best mornings of his life—without debilities
> of hangover, without pills or panic—to practice joy
> at four o'clock dawn: to test words, to break them down
> and build again, patient to construct immovable objects
> of art by the pains of intelligent attention—remaining
> alert or awake to nightmare.

Donald Hall is our finest elegist. He has, over the years, come to a vision of life not as something that begins and then ends, but as a recurrence, a seasonal reprise: "Bill Trout is incorrigible, like the recidivist blacksnake, / sparrow, and high water that turn and return in April's / versions—cycles of the same, fish making fish . . ."

A man of letters and jack-of-all-trades whose industry and catholicity have astounded the literary world for decades, Hall, author of—among many others—a prose book about baseball called *Fathers Playing Catch with Sons,* is well-known as a sports fan, specifically a baseball fan. One pictures him in his rural New Hampshire home scanning the airwaves with his satellite dish in search of games to watch:

> Baseball is not my work. It is my
> walk in the park, my pint of bitter,
> my Agatha Christie or Zane Grey—
> release of the baby animal's
> energy into the jungle gym
> of a frivolous concentration.
> Also I dictate letters between
> pitches—as I observe the Red Sox
> or whatever game's on satellite.

(Notice the nine lines, and the nine syllables per line.)

The long poem "Baseball" is couched as an attempt to explain the game to the late German collage-artist Kurt Schwitters. Not surprisingly, collage is Hall's approach here:

> The madness method
> of "Baseball" gathers bits and pieces
> of ordinary things—like bleacher
> ticket stubs, used Astroturf, Fenway
> Frank wrappers, yearbooks, and memory—
> to paste them onto the bonkers grid
> of the page.

Surprisingly, the poem is not nearly so much about baseball as it is about a dozen other strands of the poet's life: walking the dog, causeries on this and that, memories—only some of them tied to baseball. It is, not least, a frankly and enjoyably erotic poem:

> Baseball, I warrant, is not the whole
> occupation of the aging boy.
> Far from it: There are cats and roses;
> there is her water body. She fills
> the skin of her legs up, like water;
> under her blouse, water assembles,
> swelling lukewarm; her mouth is water,
> her cheekbones cool water; water flows
> in her rapid hair . . .

Listening to a baseball game on the radio a few days ago, I had a little epiphany about this poem. Then a piece in the *New York Times Book Review* by Robert Pinsky on a book by Phil Rizzuto gave words to my insight. The reason "Baseball" dwells so little on the actual game is that our involvement with the game, like Phil Rizzuto's commentary on Yankees games, "embodies," in Pinsky's words, "the divided, sometimes wandering attention, the ebbing and flowing alertness, the genial state of all-but-suspended consciousness that have made the sound of broadcast baseball a beloved national pacifier."

Hall's *Museum of Clear Ideas* gives us a taste of what our moment in time looks like through the eyes, not—as it is often presented to us—of the TV sitcom writer or the newspaper columnist, but of the sharp and even bitter satirist this poet can be. One gets a sense of how a contemporary Horace, who calls himself after a Disney character, Horace Horsecollar, would have approached our follies: the sequence is loosely modeled on Horace's odes—so loosely, in fact, that a comparison with the originals yields very little. Stanza 1 of the twenty-second of Horace's first book of odes,

> Integer vitae scelerisque purus
> non eget Mauris iaculis neque arcu
> nec venenatis gravida sagittis,
> Fusce, pharetra

(in Burton Raffel's version, "Fuscus, an honest man, / A man without guilt, / Needs no Moorish spears, / No poisoned arrows"), goes like this in Hall's rendering:

> Flaccus, drive up from Providence to see us.
> I'll buy some bargain Scotch at a New Hampshire
> liquor store and we'll celebrate your new book
>     and that good review
>
> in the *New York Times* . . .

In short, the Horatian Odes simply suggest an attitude toward, and provide occasions for commentary on, the life Hall sees going on around him. For readers familiar with the Odes, though, there are a few in-jokes. Hall has a little fun with I, 10, which Raffel translates

> Mercury, Atlantis' eloquent grandson,
> You who civilized savage man with language,
> Whose wisdom created the sandy wrestling-ground
> And gave men that gift,

by celebrating a different brand of Mercury:

> Mercury, descendant of Henry Ford's five-
> dollar-a-day Model-T factory line,
> you educated us and provided means
>     of exploration . . .

The automobile becomes "messenger of adult pleasures" and also awaits us at the end of our life's journey: "Oh, surely your transport will return again / in the procession of motors following / a sable Lincoln."

Donald Hall is interested in the generic life. Not every poet is. Reading lines like "When the young husband picked up his friend's pretty wife / in the taxi one block from her townhouse for their / first lunch together, in a hotel dining room," one may be reminded of a fiction writer like John Updike or John Cheever. Whitman's enumerations, though, give us a similar sense of the generic American life in his time:

The pure contralto sings in the organ loft,
The carpenter dresses his plank . . .
The duck-shooter walks by cautious and silent stretches,
The deacons are ordain'd with cross'd hands at the altar . . .
The connoisseur peers along the exhibition-gallery with
    half-shut eyes bent sideways . . .
The prostitute draggles her shawl, her bonnet bobs on her
    tipsy and pimpled neck . . .
The President holding a cabinet council is surrounded by
    the great secretaries.

Returning to "the young husband," Hall can sound quite the severe moralist:

                    the first
kiss with open mouths, nakedness, swoon, thrust-and-catch;
endorphins followed by endearments; a brief nap;
            another fit; restoration

of clothes, arrangements for another encounter,
the taxi back, and the furtive kiss of goodbye.
Then, by turn: tears, treachery, anger, betrayal;
            marriages and houses destroyed . . .

Horsecollar has another string to his bow, however. Following
almost all of his odes are rejoinders which a note tells us "lack
an Horatian provenance." These strike a cynical attitude that
undercuts the pathos of the odes themselves: "Or say, Why this
whining? You liked / your nooky well enough, back when / you
had your teeth."

            Do you croon guilt's anthem now
            —after twenty years of diligence
            and a gold watch—because your bald
            agent retires from the company?

At one time seemingly lost in the crowd of gifted American
poets from the celebrated "generation of '27," Donald Hall has
persisted and persevered, with the result that his poetry, rather
than standing among, now stands out. Having resigned a profes-
sorship at the University of Michigan in 1975, he has provided an

example of the poet as man of letters: essayist, editor, literary journalist, sports writer, author of children's books, critic, Dutch uncle to a generation of poets, and surely the most prolific letter-writer of his time. The remarkable thing is that, distinguished a figure as he is, Hall has managed to avoid making himself into a monument. *The Museum of Clear Ideas* is as original, idiosyncratic, and un-museumlike a poetic work as we are likely to see for a long time to come.

# James Dickey

## *The Whole Motion*

The publication of James Dickey's *The Whole Motion* finally makes available under one cover the poems he published during a career that spanned more than four decades. The extravagant imagination of the man who served up titles like *The Eye-Beaters, Blood, Victory, Madness, Buckhead,* and *Mercy* couldn't be content with something as drab as "collected poems," though the book's subtitle identifies it as such. Dickey came of age during a cultural moment when poets' reputations were often founded as much on the excesses of their personal lives as on the quality of their work. When one surveys the lives of Robert Lowell, Sylvia Plath, John Berryman, Allen Ginsberg, Randall Jarrell, Elizabeth Bishop, Theodore Roethke, and Anne Sexton, one gets the impression that mid-century American poetry somehow, with great difficulty, managed to get written between gin-fueled one-night stands in motel rooms, and recovery periods in mental hospitals and drying-out spas.

In the "lifestyle" arena, James Dickey did not disappoint. Stories about the man have become a thriving perennial in the field of literary gossip. I could without straining my memory probably tell you a dozen or more of these stories—most of them really funny, and many of them more or less true—and so, I imagine, could many readers of this book. But this is far from the only reason Dickey became the most visible Southern writer of his day. For one thing, his interest in the back-country survivalist move-

---

Review of *The Whole Motion: Collected Poems, 1945–1992* (Middletown, Conn.: Wesleyan University Press, 1994). From the *Southern Review.*

ment, in whitewater canoeing, in bow-hunting, dovetailed with regional and national rediscovery of the wilderness.

The enormously popular movie made from his novel *Deliverance* made Dickey visible to all sorts of people who don't read contemporary poetry—as well as to people who don't read much of anything other than *People* magazine, Stephen King, and *TV Guide*. When Jimmy Carter, a president who in retrospect starts to look better and better all the time, chose his fellow Georgian to deliver a poem at his inauguration, Dickey took on the ceremonial role in Washington that Robert Frost played in John F. Kennedy's presidency. By the mid-1970s Dickey had become so much of a legend that we tended to forget he was, before anything else, a superb and stunningly original poet. Few poets who began writing in the '60s—certainly few Southern poets—can credibly claim not to have been influenced by James Dickey. I gladly include myself as someone who has read, loved, and probably unconsciously imitated his poetry ever since I came under its spell some fifty years ago.

A delightful and unexpected feature of *The Whole Motion* is the inclusion of almost fifty pages of uncollected poetry written before Dickey's first book, *Into the Stone* (1960). Here we see a less flamboyant poet than the one we would come to know later, but the general outlines of his style and his ruling preoccupations are already recognizable. One of these early poems, "The Sprinter at Forty," introduces a figure Dickey will return to throughout his work: the over-the-hill athlete. Sports, competitive sports in particular, are emblematic of life and youth for this poet who often spoke proudly of his college football days at Clemson University, and wrote about them notably in "The Bee" from *Falling, May Day Sermon, and Other Poems* (1981). In "The Sprinter at Forty," the speaker states, "I receive the wish to live more / Which nothing but motion can answer" (a formulation that resonates with the word "motion" in the title of the collection). In an intellectual climate where football was thought of as a "proto-fascist" activity, Dickey's identification with the sport allowed him to put his finger on the pulse of our culture, because the competitive athlete is the American male's favorite fantasy hero. Dickey turns the superannuated athlete into a quintessentially American figure of pathos.

Dickey avoids glorifying the athlete, presenting him instead as put-upon, often injured, under attack, as in "In the Pocket," subtitled "NFL," from *Eye-Beaters* (1970): "hit move scramble," goes the quarterback's interior monologue, "Before death and the ground / Come up LEAP STAND KILL DIE STRIKE / Now." "For the Death of Lombardi," from *The Strength of Fields* (1979) shows how fully—in contrast to most other poets, who have tended to detach themselves from commercialized American culture—Dickey operated within that culture. Speaking for football fans, "those who entered the bodies / of Bart Starr, Donny Anderson, Ray Nitchke, Jerry Kramer / Through the snowing tube on Sunday afternoon," Dickey speaks for those who mourn the Green Bay Packers' legendary coach:

> We stand here among
> Discarded TV commercials:
> Among beer-cans and razor-blades and hair-tonic bottles,
> Stinking with male deodorants: we stand here
> Among teeth and filthy miles
> Of unwound tapes, Novocain needles, contracts, champagne
> Mixed with shower-water, unraveling elastic, bloody
> faceguards . . .

In *The Eagle's Mile* (1990), the celebration of "False Youth" is replayed in an overblown Whitmanian romp called "The Olympian," where, after an afternoon spent drinking Olympia beer, Dickey spoofs his own fantasy, imagining a race between himself in his "hilarious, pizza-fed fury," and an Olympic champion:

> O hot, just hurdlable gates
> Of deck-chairs! Lounges! A measured universe
> Of exhilarating laws! Here I had come there I'd gone
> Laying it down confusing, staggering
> The fast lane and the slow, on and over
> And over recliners, sun-cots, cleaning-poles and beach-balls . . .

In his early poems Dickey did not throw himself into the seductive punch-bowl of contemporary American culture. He lived and wrote at one remove from all that, in the world of his own vision. In the very first poem in the collection, "The Baggage

King," where the pile of soldiers' luggage on an island in the Pacific rises "Like the hill of a dead king," Dickey's predisposition to see demotic experience in terms of ritual announces itself. The mythic dimension in his poetry has always exercised a strong attraction for me, and it shows both his continuity with and his break from older poets such as T. S. Eliot and Allen Tate and even poets closer to his own age such as Robert Lowell. These poets were drawn explicitly to religious conversion, and tried to adumbrate their sense of larger significances lying behind everyday events by reference to classical mythology. Their evocations of the Greek and Roman myths could take the form, in Donald Hall's parodic account of the period, "of long poems in iambics called 'Herakles: A Double Sestina'"; or they could be subtle and exquisite, as in the last two quatrains of John Crowe Ransom's "Vision by Sweetwater":

> Let them alone, dear Aunt, just for one minute
> Till I go fishing in the dark of my mind:
> Where have I seen before, against the wind,
> These bright virgins, robed and bare of bonnet,

> Flowing with music of their strange quick tongue
> And adventuring with delicate paces by the stream,—
> Myself a child, old suddenly at the scream
> From one of the white throats it hid among?

The early Dickey has more in common with Ransom than meets the eye—especially since the similarities of vision are obscured by strong differences not only of diction and versification, but of intent. (Ransom was, by the way, a Cleveland Browns fan, but a poem by him on professional football is unthinkable.) Dickey never wanted to write just for the highly educated elite whom Ransom appealed to, but for the mass American audience.

But the personal myths of which I was speaking came to Dickey, it would seem, either from reading about pre-monotheistic religions and fertility cults or perhaps simply from an intuitive sense of how well their way of seeing things triggered his own imaginative thrust. Watching the movie *Black Robe*, I was reminded by a simplified description of the Algonquin version of the afterlife—"At night in the woods the souls of dead people hunt the souls of dead animals"—of Dickey's "Heaven of the Animals," where not human hunters but animals hunt other animals: "These hunt, as they have done, / But with claws and teeth grown perfect, // More deadly than they can believe." Dickey's treatment of the fate of the victims might suggest a certain callousness toward others' pain, but I think it is more accurately seen as a mystical view of the world wherein predation and suffering are subsumed within an all-inclusive unity, where

> those that are hunted
> Know this as their life,
> Their reward: to walk
>
> Under such trees in full knowledge
> Of what is in glory above them,
> And to feel no fear,
> But acceptance, compliance.
> Fulfilling themselves without pain
>
> At the cycle's center . . .

"The Owl King," one of the first Dickey poems I read, sublimates the predatory instinct in a similar way: "I felt the hooked tufts on my head / Enlarge, and dream like a crown." Here Dickey may be very close to intuiting how the raw power of feudal overlords became ritualized into the institution of kingship.

The Owl King must have represented at the same time a version of himself. I first met Dickey at the home of Monroe and Betty Spears in Sewanee, Tennessee, in about 1960, roughly the time this poem would have been written. Monroe Spears, who introduced me to modern poetry at Sewanee, was the professor at Vanderbilt whom Dickey credits with firing his enthusiasm for poetry when he entered graduate school after being discharged from the Air Force after the War. In 1960 Dickey was still writing advertising copy in Atlanta for Coca-Cola—selling his soul to the Devil by day, as he liked to put it, and buying it back at night by writing at the kitchen table of his suburban house, inventing himself as a poet. I can picture him there: "I in the innermost shining / Of my blazing, invented eyes." In "The Vegetable King," from *Into the Stone,* the poet explicitly becomes a king—the king of fertility cults, who dies with the dying year to be reborn with the spring. Here, "From my house and my silent folk / I step, and lay me in ritual down," the poet writes, "One night each April." He wills himself into ritual death and renewal, presumably at the vernal equinox, "And begin[s] to believe a dream / I never once have had / Of being part of the acclaimed rebirth / Of the ruined, calm world, in spring . . ."

Many of the poems from this period celebrate the act of willed possession, wherein the self is overtaken by the dream of kingship seen in "The Vegetable King," or where the blind child in "The Owl King" from *Drowning with Others* (1962) receives his summons, delivered in the incantatory three- and four-beat anapestic line that Dickey wrote so beautifully in his early books:

> Through the trees, with the moon underfoot,
> More soft than I can, I call.
> I hear the king of the owls sing
> Where he moves with my son in the gloom.
> My tongue floats off in the darkness . . .

This call, this summons to a transformed reality, is always, in addition to whatever else it might be, the poem's summons, the siren song of the Muse or White Goddess. Dickey makes it quite clear that the call to poetic ecstasy, like the annunciation of kingship in the fertility rite, brings with it the threat of extinction, just as the Vegetable King, returning to his wife and family, "bears you home / Magnificent pardon" but also "dread, impending crime." "A Dog Sleeping on My Feet," from *Drowning with Others,* recounts the summons specifically in terms of possession by the poem, and in an image of the crucifixion and a glancing echo of the rhetoric of the King James Bible ("Marvelous is the pursuit"), evokes the psychic peril of inspiration:

> The poem is beginning to move
> Up through my pine-prickling legs
> Out of the night wood,
>
> Taking hold of the pen by my fingers.
> Before me the fox floats lightly,
> On fire with his holy scent.
> All, all are running.

> Marvelous is the pursuit,
> Like a dazzle of nails through the ankles . . .

It may be that Dickey's greatest work still lay ahead of him at this point, but I wonder if he ever again achieved the exquisite purity, the Botticelli-like sense of sanctity, of the poems he wrote in the late-night isolation of the Atlanta suburbs. Dickey's uncollected early poems make clear how essential this kind of psychic self-immolation (I feel uncomfortable with my own ponderous language here, but it's hard to put it more simply) was to Dickey in the early days. "Drifting," a marvelous poem I had never seen before, dramatizes the process of leaving the self behind—using a metaphor perhaps borrowed from Rimbaud's *Le Bateau ivre:*

> It is worth it to get
> Down there under the seats, stretched believingly out
> With your feet together,
>
> Thinking of nothing but the smell of bait and the sky
> And the bow coming
> To a point and the stern squared off until doomsday.

The metaphor may be Rimbaud's, but the details are very Southern, with the idiomatic overload of prepositions in "get / Down there under the seats" and the grandeur of the viewed sky undermined by the "smell of bait." Rimbaud in a bass boat!

If you can imagine this poem in the oeuvre of one of his contemporaries—Sylvia Plath, John Berryman, or Anne Sexton, to construct an implausible "for instance"—then this voyage would suggest suicide:

> Once in a lifetime a man must empty his pockets
> On the bank of a river,
> Take out two monogrammed handkerchiefs and tie them
>
> To the oars stuck in the sand:
> These mark the edge of the known . . .

This represents no death wish, however, but rather the poet's wish to leave the personality behind, and to float as Keats does—"Not charioted by Bacchus and his pards, / But on the viewless wings of Poesy."

If one thinks of Dickey's suburban pastoral as an idyll he entered gladly, gratefully, after the war, still the war continued to haunt him—a process that is especially clear in *Helmets* (1964). In the poem "Drinking from a Helmet," the GI poet, by drinking from the helmet of a man he imagines to have been killed, takes on that man's identity: "I stood as though I possessed / A cool, trembling man / Exactly my size, swallowed whole." This is an image of the warrior who must go back to his peacetime world and live the life of the civilian, all the time carrying within him the man who has fought, has managed to avoid being killed, has himself perhaps killed.

In *Buckdancer's Choice,* winner of the National Book Award in 1965, the third of the astonishing trio of books that began in 1962 with *Drowning with Others,* Dickey addresses the dilemma of the returned warrior in one of his most controversial poems, eight pages long, "The Firebombing." The speaker in the poem, a comfortable yet uneasy suburbanite, tries in the midst of a typical middle-class life spent paying bills, mowing the lawn, fretting about his receding hairline, to come to terms with his experiences as a World War II pilot who carried out "anti-morale" napalm bombing runs against Japanese civilian targets. Memories of the firebombings intrude themselves at the edges of quotidian concerns, cropping up as "fire" in the word "firewood" does in a broken line in this passage that describes his suburban home: "Where the lawn mower rests on its laurels"—the clichéd wording hinting at its owner's less than acute state of mind—

> Where the diet exists
> For my own good where I try to drop
> Twenty years, eating figs in the pantry
> Blinded by each and all
> Of the eye-catching cans that gladly have caught my wife's eye
> Until I cannot say
> Where the screwdriver is where the children
> Get off the bus where the fly
> Hones his front legs where the hammock folds
> Its erotic daydreams where the Sunday
> School text for the day has been put where the fire

Wood is where the payments
For everything under the sun
Pile peacefully up . . .

In 1967 Robert Bly, speaking from the pulpit of his influential magazine, *The Sixties,* castigated the poem in a vitriolic essay called "The Collapse of James Dickey." His main contention was that "'Firebombing'"—note how leaving "The" out of the title changes its meaning—"makes no real criticism of the American habit of firebombing Asians." Bly was demanding that the poem's subject should be not the ambivalence felt by one particular pilot toward his own actions, but rather that the poem become a kind of editorial against all American military action in Asia, with the premise that the war in the South Pacific against the Japanese was identical to the war against Vietnam. Dickey once wrote that we live "in the age of the moral putdown," and after attacks like Bly's, he was in a position to know. In abandoning any notion of aesthetic evaluation of poetry and insisting it become propaganda for the critic's political beliefs, Bly was ahead of his time—since his approach would soon become dogma in academia. Bly condemns the poem because it displays "no real anguish. If the anguish were real, we would feel terrible remorse as we read, we would stop what we were doing, we would break the television set with an ax, we would throw ourselves on the ground sobbing."

I have addressed myself mainly to poems from the first part of Dickey's *Whole Motion*—the first 240 pages of a 475-page collection—because these are the poems that speak to me most strongly. While writing this piece I have reached down my original Wesleyan Poetry Series paperbacks of *Drowning with Others, Helmets,* and *Buckdancer's Choice* to remind me of the sense of discovery I got reading these books when they first appeared. Even the atrocious cover art of these books bespeaks an awkward sincerity, reminiscent of Baptist Sunday-school teachers' instruction manuals. I have never been as enthusiastic about Dickey's work from *Falling, May Day Sermon, and Other Poems* on, as I continue to be about the early work. In his introduction to *Falling, May Day Sermon, and Other Poems,* Dickey writes of designing "an on-end block or wall of words, solid or almost solid, black with massed ink, through which a little light from behind would come at intermittent places." And that for me is part of the problem. The wall of words, like the famous "wall of sound" introduced into Top Forty music by Phil Spector, seems to sacrifice some of the quieter, more subtle effects Dickey achieved when he was writing earlier.

In poems like "Falling," Dickey tries to imitate a motion whose sweep outruns the ability of his language to keep up with it. "The Sheep Child," one of his most notorious poems, narrated by a dead half-human, half-sheep fetus pickled in alcohol in a museum in Atlanta, strikes me as Southern grotesquerie gone over the limit. "Adultery," on the other hand, dares to tread the same fine line between originality and questionable moral taste (or am I sounding like Robert Bly?); yet it succeeds, because one thing that Dickey is not, is a hypocrite. "Encounter in the Cage Country" continues this remarkable poet's intuitive interaction with the natural world, but I prefer the poems where Dickey goes out to meet the animals on their own turf, not in the London zoo. Maybe I heard too many sermons when I was a boy, but I flip the pages of "May Day Sermon to the Women of Gilmer County, Georgia, by a Woman Preacher Leaving the Baptist Church" just as I flip my car radio dial past the Sunday-morning sermons I come across. "The Zodiac" may capture with perfect verisimilitude the drunken ravings of a poet with an unusual imagination; but I've been there myself sufficiently often to know that a little of it goes a long way.

Having said that, and having not even ventured a glance in the direction of Dickey's achievements as a literary critic and novelist, I think there are many fine things in the later parts of *The Whole Motion*. Dickey's elegy for Vince Lombardi I have already cited. "The Rain Guitar" from *The Strength of Fields,* where Dickey sits out in the rain by an English stream near Winchester Cathedral playing the guitar (he is a virtuoso picker) while an Englishman with a wooden leg casts for trout, is as tight, as inspired, as jaunty, as anything he ever wrote. The poem ends:

> I was Air Force,
> I said. So was I; I picked
> This up in Burma, he said, tapping his gone leg

With his fly rod, as Burma and the South
west Pacific and North Georgia reeled,
Rapped, cast, chimed, darkened and drew down
Cathedral water, and improved.

The reeling (of the fly reel, and the reel Dickey is playing on the guitar), the rapping (on the wooden leg, as well as the word in its '60s sense), the chiming (of the two men's war experiences, along with the cathedral bells), synchronize magically.

As I remember this brilliant, flawed man, I like to image him, in a poet's afterlife, continuing to stand out in thunderstorms, open to the lightning-strike of inspiration, wearing his famous denim jacket with the eagle embroidered on it, so that we, like the barbershop rednecks in "False Youth: Autumn Clothes of the Age," can

> get a lifetime look at my bird's
One word, raggedly blazing with extinction and soaring loose
In red threads burning up white until I am shot in the back
Through my wings or ripped apart
For rags . . .

# The Life and Fables of Bob Dylan

Coming through the radio of the car you drove cross-country to
California, loud on the phonograph in somebody's East Village
apartment, threading through the years and the series of events
we have agreed to call The Sixties—which encompassed "folk"
music, the Movement, the half-decade of assassinations that
started in Dallas and ended in Los Angeles, the tune-in turn-on
drop-out phase, the Revolution that wasn't—Bob Dylan's sand-
papery, nasal, insistent voice can be heard, asking his generation's questions, assaulting us with instances of injustice in our
country, persisting in his harrowing pursuit of true and ideal
love. Dylan did more than give voice to common concerns; he
like Hemingway guided us to new areas of experience and even
influenced how we would react once we got there: "You know
something's happening, but you don't know what it is. Do you,
Mister Jones?" (We need to hear Dylan's sneering voice and
Robbie Robertson's guitar behind these words. Print is too cold
a medium to present them in.)

While the songs of Woody Guthrie and the prose of Jack Kerouac accompanied well-brought-up Bobby Zimmerman, son of
an appliance-store owner and Rotarian in Hibbing, Minnesota,
to Duluth, to Minneapolis, and ultimately to New York City, the
records he made there under the name Bob Dylan were in turn
a powerful education for other middle-class kids who were just
waking up to the military-industrial complex, the cruelties of
racial segregation, and the Wonder Bread texture of Ozzie-and-
Harriet America. Dylan would later recoil from being labeled a

Review of *No Direction Home: The Life and Music of Bob Dylan,* by Robert
Shelton (New York: Beech Tree Books, 1986). Earlier versions appeared in the *Michigan Quarterly Review* and the *Missouri Review.*

"protest" singer, but that was where he started—as a perceptive social critic with a gift for burlesquing the objects of his scorn:

> Where Ma Rainey and Beethoven once unwrapped a
> bedroll,
> Tuba players now rehearse around the flagpole.
> And the National Bank at a profit sells road maps for the
> soul
> To the Old Folks' Home and the College.
>
> ("Tombstone Blues")

Righteous indignation, a sense of what was funny and what was not, a finely tuned bullshit detector, a predilection for what his biographer Robert Shelton, in *No Direction Home: The Life and Music of Bob Dylan,* calls the "truth attack"—these qualities made Dylan an indispensable ally and guide for those who were setting out to liberate themselves from that cross-indexed catchall, the System.

Even when the heat of the 1960s simmered down about halfway through the '70s, Dylan's songs still spoke to and about those he called "the crowd of people who were on the same wavelength I was on," the hip elite, the activists, the dropouts:

> All the people we used to know,
> They're an illusion to me now.
> Some are mathematicians, some are carpenters' wives.
> Don't know how it all got started,
> I don't know what they're doing with their lives.
>
> ("Tangled Up in Blue")

The enterprise of coming down off the communal acid-trip, dropping back in, wiping the strangeness from one's eyes, and retooling for re-entry into the American mainstream had its own poignancy. *Blood on the Tracks* (1975) and *Desire* (1976), which chronicled re-entry, were among Dylan's most moving performances.

Later, Dylan's conversion to born-again Christianity, while not an anomaly within the life of someone who has tended to see life in religious terms all along, was an enthusiasm most of his fans were not inclined to share. Yet at least one song from that period, the gospel-inspired "Gotta Serve Somebody," with its brilliant particulars, its drive, its chorus of black women backing up Dylan's panoramic social catalog, is a classic. Here is one verse from it (please listen to this and my other examples from Dylan if you have the recordings and the time):

> You may be a construction worker, working on a home.
> You might be living in a mansion, you might live in a dome.
> You may own guns, you may even own tanks.
> You may be somebody's landlord, you may even own banks.
> But you're gonna have to serve somebody.
> It may be the Devil or it may be the Lord,
> But you're gonna have to serve somebody.

To begin at the beginning: Like many another American teenager, Bobby Zimmerman dreamed of becoming a rock 'n' roll star. He put together teenage bands with names like the Golden Chords and the Satin Tones, and filled Hibbing's rec halls and garages and gymnasiums—whenever he could get somebody to listen—with echoes of Elvis Presley and Buddy Holly. But by the time Dylan had dropped out of the University of Minnesota and was living the beatnik life in Minneapolis, rock bore the stigma of all things mainstream commercial American. "Folk music" was something different. A folksinger was someone with a name like Woody Guthrie or Cisco Houston or Leadbelly or Blind Lemon Jefferson, who rode the rails every chance he got, sang union songs on picket lines or blues songs in brothels, picked grapes alongside migrant workers in California, and just generally did the things that a legend in his own time would do.

Zimmerman set about creating a legendary character known as Bob Dylan (the name perhaps owed as much to *Gunsmoke*'s Matt Dillon as to Dylan Thomas). Dylan had acquired a very serviceable folksinger's background by the time he got off the subway at Sheridan Square. In 1960 he "burst on the scene already a legend, the / unwashed phenomenon, the original vagabond," as Joan Baez described him years later in her song "Diamonds and Rust." (Years earlier he had written "Visions of Joanna" in reference to her.) The song goes on to raise the spectre of the madonna or muse who is at the heart of much of Dylan's writing:

> You strayed into my arms
> And there you stayed, temporarily lost at sea.
> The madonna was yours for free,
> Yes the girl on the half-shell
> Could keep you unharmed.

In pursuit of the myth he was creating around himself, here is the résumé he gave to Izzy Young, proprietor of the Folklore Center on MacDougal Street, where the urban folksingers hung out, learned new songs, and refined their guitar-licks while fantasizing about adventures "out there" in America:

> Played piano with Bobby Vee—would've been a millionaire if I'd stayed with him . . . Before I met Jesse Fuller in Denver, there was a farmhand in Sioux Falls, South Dakota, who played the autoharp . . . Cowboy styles I learned from real cowboys. Can't remember their names. Met some in Cheyenne . . .

Yet Dylan seems to have had mixed feelings about the talkin'-union, workshirt-wearin' folksinger shtick, and he parodied the style by making up noms de guitare for himself like Blind Boy Grunt. Here are some impressions of young Bob Dylan, apple-cheeked, newly arrived from Minnesota:

> Bob just seemed a kid, somehow, quite nervous when he wasn't singing and playing, doing a perpetual little dance with his boot toes, even seated . . . But there was a tremendous transformation when he started playing. One was astonished to hear that kind of driving playing on guitar and powerful singing voice coming from a kid who hadn't even started growing a beard. I frankly was baffled by the discrepancy, and harbored the impression for a while that he was somehow putting us on, taking us in. I thought some of his songs were deliberate takeoffs on folk songs, hoaxes . . . I thought: "Who is he trying to kid?" But you couldn't tell from his facial expression.

When "Blowin' in the Wind" became an inspiration to the Movement, it was clear to everyone that this was a Civil Rights song, an anthem if you will, like the Beatles' "All You Need Is

Love" and the Youngbloods' "Get Together." If one listens to the words today, the song seems equally to be rather straightforwardly about growing up:

> How many roads must a man walk down
> Before they call him a man?
> How many seas must a white dove sail
> Before she sleeps in the sand?

Two points are worth making. One, Dylan succeeded in identifying the struggle of blacks for social and economic equality with the struggle of young whites, himself definitely included, for their own empowerment as adults. His songs spoke for both struggles. That's what made the songs work, and that's what made the Movement succeed to the extent that it did accomplish something. Two, on the subject of Dylan as folksinger: there was a slot for him in that capacity. It was a one-man opportunity, which was easier than putting together a band, as he would probably have preferred to do. He had neither the voice, the experience, nor the contacts to become a rock 'n' roll star (this would come later). But since he wrote lyrics of great power, supplemented his eccentric voice with resourceful guitar and harmonica, and was at the same time a standup comedian of originality and charm, the world was ready to hand him a live microphone.

Dylan was an accomplished mimic, and like anyone in search of a viable identity, he found many models. Even in his Minneapolis days, as one observer put it, "Every few weeks, Bob would become a different person with a different style." One of his early New York idols was the cowboy folksinger Ramblin' Jack Elliott. Ramblin' Jack actually knew Woody Guthrie, while Dylan had just managed to visit him in the hospital and play him a song. Few people were aware that Ramblin' Jack Elliott had been born Charles Adnopoz, a physician's son from a "fifteen-thousand-acre ranch in the middle of Flatbush." Except in song, he had never punched a cow or urged little dogies to get along. Shelton tells of the time folksinger Dave Van Ronk and music publisher Barry Kornfeld clued Dylan in to Ramblin' Jack's bona fides: "When they referred to Elliott's being a Jewish cowboy from Brooklyn, Van Ronk said, 'Bobby nearly fell off his chair laughing. It seemed to strike him much funnier than it did us . . .'"

Dylan absorbed so much of Elliott that today if you should happen to hear Ramblin' Jack on the coffeehouse circuit, you could swear he was imitating the Freewheelin' Bob Dylan. But Dylan has remained a maker and wearer of masks. His album *Self Portrait* (1970) consists almost entirely of songs by other people. His pictures never look the same from album cover to album cover. His voice has been much derided (*bel canto* it is not), but it too changes expressively from album to album and is capable of widely varying tones and moods.

To stress Dylan's mercurial nature (astrology experts make much of his being a double Gemini), is not to agree with those who feel his early commitment to social protest was a put-on or a calculated career-move. In fact his mixed feelings about being a spokesman for the Old Left, the New Left, or any other movement, say something in favor of his personal integrity. With his songs Dylan really did help strike a blow against racism, really did help mobilize tangible resistance against militarism. It is true that all songs take some of their meaning from the milieux in which they are sung. "As Time Goes By" means something different within the cinematic confines of Rick's American Café than it does when performed at Cousin Howard's wedding reception at the Holiday Inn. However ambiguous the words of the song might seem in retrospect, "Blowin' in the Wind," when sung by Dylan, or by Mary Travers of Peter, Paul and Mary, her long blond hair unbound, at an open-air protest rally, meant something very close to "We Shall Overcome."

Years later, Dylan would tell the architect of his house in Malibu that he "wanted a living room he could ride a horse through," yet his sympathy for the underdog was genuine, and it was not just sympathy but identification. As is fitting for a practitioner of vernacular American music, with its crucial African American component, Dylan has shown a rare empathy for the position of American blacks. The notorious speech he made to the "Old Left burghers" who presented him with the Tom Paine Award in December 1963 illustrates how different Dylan's anarchic radicalism was from the sentimental views of the people who were sitting around eating steaks and talking about the Spanish Civil War:

> There's not black and white, left and right to me anymore, there's only up and down, and down is very close to the ground . . . I got to admit that the man who shot President Kennedy, Lee Oswald . . . I don't know what he thought he was doing, but I got to admit honestly that I, too—I saw something of myself in him.

This was less than a month after the assassination. Dylan was reportedly smashed at the time he made these remarks, but they show a man determined not to be the puppet of any political camp, and more importantly, a man whose thinking, in its unprogrammed rawness, is instinctively much closer to the popular mind than to the pieties of his sponsors.

Dylan's "betrayal" of the Left is as much a non-issue as was his "betrayal" of acoustic folk music. In both cases he was the victim of a stereotype other people wanted to impose on him. Another non-issue is whether Dylan is a poet. Of course he is. He is an oral poet. Academic critics have tried to resolve this issue by typing up Dylan's lyrics and asking whether they "stand up" as poetry. Since song lyrics have to be apprehended by the ear, which also experiences the total song, appreciating how the words and music support and enhance each other, it is quite irrelevant how the lyrics read on the page. John Ashbery's poems don't come with playable MPG files. Dylan is certainly a poet in the big sense: he has moved people by the beauty of his songs, he has often moved them to action, and he has revitalized the Word for many purposes it may have lost while confined to the page. Dylan has not been just another showbiz phenomenon, another Frank Sinatra, another Elvis Presley. Dylan, at least for those who appreciate him, has fulfilled a role for which there is only the embarrassing word Bard. Peculiarly, he has used the paraphernalia of showbiz to accomplish this.

Here the late Albert Grossman, Dylan's Mephistophelean business manager, enters the picture. If Dylan occasionally plays Christ in his songs, then Grossman was his Judas. But the two men had much in common, according to Robert Shelton: "Bob and Albert's strange, often stormy relationship was in some ways a true marriage of minds and temperaments, each quickly adopting the worst traits of the other. The striking difference was that Bob had appeared to be a relatively open person with considerable human compassion, while Albert had always been the chess player."

Grossman had a master's degree in economics from the University of Chicago, and had studied child psychology with Bruno Bettelheim. Shelton shows how these two fields of study found a rather ominous synthesis in Grossman: "As a trained economic theorist and a semi-trained child psychologist, Albert became one of the most powerful managers in 1960s show business." Grossman promoted Dylan ruthlessly and assisted him in making a fortune, while lurking in the shadows of Dylan's success as an eminence grise. "Next to Albert," Peter Yarrow is quoted as saying, "Dylan was an amateur at cutting people down. Albert is an expert at destroying other people's sense of self. He readily admits it."

Dylan's sense of self was already fragile; he had achieved negative capability in excess, particularly in the period just before his catastrophic motorcycle accident in 1966. At least two songs on *John Wesley Harding* (1968), his first album following the accident and his ensuing period of seclusion, seem to refer to Dylan's association with his manager, turning an incident from his personal life into fable. (Grossman's response to the accident was: "How could he do this to me?") In "The Ballad of Frankie Lee and Judas Priest" we see Judas lending Frankie Lee money:

> Well Frankie Lee and Judas Priest,
> They were the best of friends.
> So when Frankie Lee needed money one day,
> Judas quickly pulled out a roll of tens
>
> And placed them on a footstool
> Just above the clouded plain,
> Saying "Take your pick, Frankie Boy.
> My loss will be your gain."

As the story unfolds, Judas Priest summons Frankie Lee down the road to a house (only "'It's not a house,' said Judas Priest. 'It's not a house, it's a home'") with "four-and-twenty windows / And a woman's face in every one." Already in debt to Judas, Frankie Lee approaches the women who've been presented to him, and sets out to "make his midnight creep":

> For sixteen nights and days he made,
> But on the seventeenth he burst
> Into the arms of Judas Priest,
> Which is where he died of thirst.
>
> No one tried to say a thing
> When they carried him out in jest—
> Except of course the little neighbor boy
> Who carried him to rest.
>
> And he just walked along alone
> With his guilt so well concealed,
> And muttered underneath his breath,
> "Nothing is revealed."

The song is a haunting one. Dylan recites the lines, rather than singing them, with an incongruous air of preciseness and facetiousness. It's a murky fable of misplaced trust and subsequent betrayal. Judas Priest at first calls his house "Eternity," then hedges: "Though you might call it Paradise." "I don't call it anything," Frankie Lee replies. At the end of the song Frankie Lee is dead, and Dylan warns us, perhaps facetiously, "Don't go mistaking paradise / For that home across the road."

One of the lines I have quoted, "Nothing is revealed," could well be Dylan's motto, for like contemporary poets John Ashbery and James Tate, Dylan's stock-in-trade is the baffling surface, the straight face, the sense of significance concealed beneath a matter-of-fact or nonsensical cover. A listener is seldom sure he or she is on solid ground, and that's part of the appeal. "Dear Landlord," from the same album, would appear to comment incisively on the relationship between the artist and his manager—and more largely, of course, on a subject Dylan with all his success was uniquely positioned to contemplate: the symbiosis of art and commerce.

Dear Landlord, please don't put a price on my soul.
My burden is heavy, my dreams are beyond control.
When that steamboat whistle blows,
I'm gonna give you all I've got to give.
And I do hope you receive it well,
Depending on the way you feel that you live.

I mentioned earlier the idea of Dylan as Christ and his manager as Judas. Admittedly the subject of Christ-figures has become a hackneyed one. But in this case it, in the words of the old gospel song, is "so high I can't get over it, so low I can't get under it, so wide I can't get around it." The rock 'n' roll poets of the '60s, whose records were listened to, literally, religiously, had as their audience a close-knit subculture who regarded the peak years of the '60s and early '70s as a "trip," a sequence of meaningful events, experienced communally. Dylan, the Stones, the Beatles, even a featherweight like Donovan, specialized in veiled messages—initially about pot and acid, later about social events, etc.—directed specifically at their peer-group.

With organized religion having lost its authority, with widespread cynicism about politics, and the few charismatic leaders on the scene falling victim to assassination, the Beatles became, as John Lennon provocatively claimed, more popular than Jesus Christ. And this was even more true of Dylan. The power, the pressure of having millions of people turning to you for direction, is hard for the average person to appreciate. Lennon sang—prophetically, it turned out—"The way things are going, / They're gonna crucify me"; and Dylan was also very aware of the public's frightening habit of elevating a leader or star to a near-divine position (like Martin Luther King's "mountaintop") and then cutting him down. The early Dylan was obsessed with death, and after the motorcycle crash and period of withdrawal following it, images of death-and-rebirth became common in his songs.

In "Shelter from the Storm," from *Blood on the Tracks*, he makes a characteristic reference to reincarnation and his encounter with his *anima* or muse:

'Twas in another lifetime,
One of toil and blood,
When blackness was a virtue,

> The road was full of mud.
> I came in from the wilderness,
> A creature void of form.
> "Come in," she said, "I'll give you
> Shelter from the storm."

As the story develops, the singer-protagonist appears to be in a position analogous to Christ's, alive after the Crucifixion. The woman "walked up to me so gracefully / And took my crown of thorns," providing him a refuge after his ordeal. Another way of looking at it is that the story of Christ serves as a metaphor for an autobiographical story. Certainly there is a note of bitterness and, again, a sense of having been betrayed:

> In a little hilltop village
> They gambled for my clothes.
> I bargained for salvation
> And she gave me a lethal dose.
> I offered up my innocence,
> Got repaid with scorn.
> "Come in," she said, "I'll give you
> Shelter from the storm."

Dylan's imagination is powerfully energized by myth. He thinks on the level of myth. Death and rebirth are always connected in his songs with the muse or female double: listen to "Isis" and "Tangled Up in Blue" and "Simple Twist of Fate," more superb songs from *Blood on the Tracks,* where Dylan uses the same short, thematic refrain as in "Shelter from the Storm" to tie up the diverse threads of narrative. Both Jung's writing on the *anima* and Robert Graves's White Goddess shed light on Dylan's female myths. Here's the story in one couplet, from "Oh Sister": "We grew up together from the cradle to the grave. / We died and were reborn and left mysteriously saved."

The search for this other self, twin, muse, madonna, has turned out to be a strikingly insistent quest for Dylan. Though he is sardonic and a master of the put-on, this is one subject he has not tended to joke about. And over the long haul this lady has not proved, contrary to the words of Joan Baez's song about her old lover, to be his "for free."

Dylan's early songs addressed to women are, like his early songs addressed to everyone else, confrontational and derisive. "Just Like a Woman," for example, takes for its title a traditionally derogative male comment. The emotions run deep here, but they are bittersweet:

> It was raining from the first, and I was dying of thirst,
> So I came in here.
> Your longtime curse hurts, but what's worse
> Is this pain in here. I can't stay in here,
> Ain't it clear?
> That I just can't fit.
> Yes I believe it's time for us to quit.
> And when we meet again, introduced as friends,
> Please don't let on that you knew me when
> I was hungry and it was your world.

Standing out among the hard-edged, hyper-excited songs on the 1966 album *Blonde on Blonde,* where "Just Like a Woman" also appears, "Sad-Eyed Lady of the Lowlands" takes up one whole side of a record and is a hymnlike wedding song to his wife Sara, whom he married in 1965. At that stage in Dylan's career it was a bit of a shock to hear him getting this mellow. These are song lyrics, meant to be heard, so listen to the record if you have it. The printed words don't convey their full effect, but the band Dylan assembled in the Columbia studios in Nashville, with Kenny Buttrey's measured drumming and Al Kooper's lush organ, backed up a Dylan who for once sounded fulfilled and at peace:

> With your mercury mouth in the Missionary Times,
> And your eyes like smoke and your prayers like rhymes,
> And your silver cross and your voice like chimes,
> Oh who did they think could come bury you?

Here he lays out his gifts in the traditional manner at the lady's feet: "My warehouse eyes, my Arabian drums: / Should I leave them by your gate, / Or sad-eyed lady, should I wait?"

Like many writers who present an autobiographical surface, Dylan works with the illusion of an actual life—autobiography as a poetic convenience, a resource, a vehicle for communication with an audience. "I" really *can* be "another," and particularly for people who create lyrics and tell stories, the self is no fixed commodity.

One key to the magnetism of Dylan's songs is his ability to lose himself in his material, to exercise negative capability. In daily life this capacity has, as Aristotle would say, the defects of its qualities. Dylan has often been lost. His song "Too Much of Nothing" makes that clear.

Perhaps the absence of a fixed self makes his search for the spiritualized, feminine ideal standing behind many real women all the more urgent for him. His best songs of intensely romantic, star-crossed love appear on *Blood on the Tracks* and *Desire*, coinciding with the breakup of his marriage to the woman for whom he wrote "Sad-Eyed Lady of the Lowlands." The lady in one of my favorite Dylan songs, "Tangled Up in Blue," is not the usual dark-eyed, dark-haired beauty, but a redhead:

> Early one morning the sun was shining,
> I was laying in bed,
> Wondering if she'd changed at all,
> If her hair was still red.
> Her folks they said our lives together
> Sure was gonna be rough.
> They never did like Mama's homemade dress,
> Papa's bankbook wasn't big enough.

The song recounts the adventures, split-ups, and reunions of this couple, separated by circumstance and reunited by fate. But after you listen a few times, you sense that all these stories couldn't have involved the same woman. This romance must be a composite. And Dylan hints at the poet-muse connection when the woman, whom he has at this point rediscovered working in a topless place—"I must admit I felt a little uneasy / When she bent down to tie the lace of my shoe"—in New Orleans, takes him to her apartment, "lit a burner on the stove / And offered me a pipe," then hands him a book of poems by "an Italian poet / From the thirteenth century." Who else could it be but Dante, whose love for Beatrice is the quintessential story of the poet's attachment to his muse? The poetry brings an instant shock of recognition:

> And every one of those words rang true
> And glowed like burning coals,
> Pouring off of every page
> Like it was written in my soul,
> Brought me to you,
> Tangled up in blue.

Blue is the blue of her eyes, a blue mood, blue of the sky—and then there's Dylan's earlier song "It's All Over Now, Baby Blue," which starts one thinking about recurring characters in Dylan's body of work.

"Simple Twist of Fate," the next track after "Tangled Up in Blue," tells of an encounter, seemingly casual, on the waterfront somewhere—a one-night stand that leaves him with "an emptiness inside." So he goes looking for this woman, walking by the docks, "where the sailors all come in. / Maybe she'll pick him out again. / How long must he wait / One more time for a simple twist of fate?" The song fudges beautifully on point of view, sliding meaningfully out of the third person to show that he was the "he" in the song: "They walked along by the old canal / A little confused, I remember well." In the last stanza of this haunting song, Dylan drops all pretense that it's a story about someone else:

> People tell me it's a sin
> To know and feel too much within.
> I still believe she was my twin,
> But I lost the ring . . .

These songs mingle rapture and regret, and there is an air of poignant sadness to them. The series is topped off by "Sara" from *Desire,* an elegiac song that marks the end of his twelve-year marriage, a gesture as final and as painful as the ten-million-dollar divorce settlement.

Dylan is one of our truest poets—though literary critics uncomfortable with an aural medium shy away from discussing him as the poet he is. The pervading presence of ambiguity in his songs is of more than passing interest within a poetic zeit-geist where ambiguity has been so highly valued. A chapter on Dylan would have made a nice conclusion to William Empson's classic *Seven Types of Ambiguity*. It's fascinating though not surprising to see that over the course of his career social themes easily lost out to eros and the encounter with the muse. How consistent this is with Robert Graves's classic account of the poet's encounter with the White Goddess in his poem "To Juan at the Winter Solstice":

> Dwell on her graciousness, dwell on her smiling,
> Do not forget what flowers
> The great boar trampled down in ivy time.
> Her brow was creamy as the crested wave,
> Her sea-blue eyes were wild
> But nothing promised that is not performed.

# John Crowe Ransom

*Tennessee's Major Minor Poet*

For a generation of readers influenced by the literary criticism of T. S. Eliot, the distinction between "major" and "minor" poets is an accepted commonplace. The implication is that a major poet is somehow better than a minor. Many of us, however, reserve a valued place in our reading lives for the "great minor poet"—someone whose work is of the highest distinction, is original and memorable and gives great pleasure, but who lacks the grand ambition to make, like Milton or Dante, a major philosophical or religious statement; to define, as Homer, Virgil, Chaucer, Shakespeare, Yeats, and Whitman did, an epoch or a national or ethnic identity.

It can be a relief to turn from these top-heavy, "major" goliaths to artists we think of as minor. Samuel Johnson took the measure not only of Milton but of other literary greats when he wrote: *"Paradise Lost* is one of the books which the reader admires and lays down, and forgets to take up again. None ever wished it longer than it is." "Minor" poets escape some of the burdens associated with the ambition to be great, and often their verse is purer and more pleasurable as a result. They seem content to go about the business of writing poems, doing justice to what they perceive and intuit, creating objects of delight and insight without laboring under the burden of explaining history, defining the national psyche, or awing us with their "genius."

Review of *Selected Poems* (New York: Knopf, 1991) and *Gentleman in a Dustcoat: A Biography of John Crowe Ransom,* by Thomas Daniel Young (Baton Rouge: Louisiana State University Press, 1977). From the *New Criterion.*

Every lover of poetry will have his or her own list of favorites. My own short and incomplete list would include several names from the English Renaissance—Robert Herrick, George Herbert, Andrew Marvell—and several Americans, including Robinson Jeffers, Theodore Roethke, Marianne Moore, Elizabeth Bishop. Among the modern English, Philip Larkin, Ted Hughes, Stevie Smith, and U. A. Fanthorpe. Among the Irish, Louis MacNiece, Michael Longley, and Derek Mahon.

Near the top of my list of great minor poets would be John Crowe Ransom (1888–1974), who published fewer than 160 poems, whittling that number down to 80 in his *Selected Poems*. He was active as a poet for about eleven years, between 1916 and 1927.

As a critic, Ransom was in no doubt as to where he stood on the major/minor question. He agreed with what his friend Allen Tate wrote in a letter in 1926: "I'm afraid Eliot is about right in saying there are no important themes for modern poets, hence we all write lyrics." In 1938, in his critical book *The World's Body,* he pointedly defends the genre:

> The virtue of formal lyrics, or "minor poems," is one that no other literary type can manifest: they are the only complete and self-determined poetry. There the poetic object is elected by a free choice from all objects in the world, and this object, deliberately elected and carefully worked up by the adult poet, becomes his microcosm. With a serious poet each minor poem may be a symbol of a major decision: it is as ranging and comprehensive an action as the mind has ever tried.

Ransom wrote, at his best, with unexampled serenity and mastery. For the student of metrics, the way his line employs traditional English meter without becoming monotonous never ceases to amaze. In the opening quatrain of "Blue Girls," the first three lines, though they are in iambic pentameter, all begin with an accent rather than the expected unaccented first syllable of the iamb. The last line contains only three beats. Because of the way the lines begin with "strong attack" (propelled metrically by the spondee or trochee) and because of the shorter last line, the stanza glancingly alludes to the classical Sapphic stanza; yet the

ABBA rhyme scheme, associated with Tennyson's *In Memoriam,* suggests an elegiac tone.

You can appreciate the genius of Ransom's rhythms by artificially marking out the first two lines as if they followed the strict iambic pentameter meter (they do not). The first line has the expected ten syllables; the second is the same, with an extra unstressed syllable giving the line a feminine ending:

> \* /   \*   /   \*   / \* /   \*   /
> Twirling your blue skirts, travelling the sward,
> \*   /   \* / \* / \*   / \* / \*
> Under the towers of your seminary . . .

That stilted and deliberately tin-eared scansion gives the norm, the base meter against which Ransom and all the other great metricists—including Shakespeare, Milton, Pope, Keats, Yeats, Frost, and Auden—work. (To readers with a well-developed ear, as well as anyone who has ever read Paul Fussell's little gem, *Poetic Meter and Poetic Form,* this is all commonplace. I apologize to them: they are few in number.) Here's how the line really goes:

> / \*   \*   /   /   / \* \*   \*   /
> Twirling your blue skirts, travelling the sward
> /   \*   \* /   \* \* \*   / \* /   \*
> Under the towers of your seminary,
> / / \*   \* \*   /   \*   /   \*   \*   / \*
> Go listen to your teachers old and contrary
> \* /   \* / \*   \*   /
> Without believing a word.

Part of the beauty of the first line lies in the spondaic effect of "blue skirts" followed, after the caesura or pause, by the additional accent that occurs in the first syllable of "travelling," the last two syllables of which a good reader wants to elide for the sake of the phrasing. The line is a little rhythmical unit with two almost identical phrases, each beginning with the same consonant sound and each suggesting a triplet rhythm, like a measure of music with a triplet laid across the 4/4 meter. (The first line of the second stanza echoes that rhythm, though not exactly,

47

with "white" and the first syllable of "fillets" echoing "blue skirts," and "then" providing the accent that begins the second half-line.) The third line attacks strongly, its imperative emphasized by the spondee in the first foot—"Go listen"—and ending with the graceful feminine ending on "seminary"—an old-fashioned name for a private school, not necessarily suggesting a school of theology. The last line has a very strong anapestic (∗ ∗ /) feeling. Here's the second stanza unsullied by scansion markings:

> Tie the white fillets then about your hair
> And think no more of what will come to pass
> Than bluebirds that go walking on the grass
> And chattering on the air.

The "fillets," or headbands, will make readers with some memory of the Latin poetry they read in school think of the stylized fasciae of the maidens that grace classical verse.

At the same time that the poem stirs up whatever latent memories we might have of classical poetry, "come to pass" alludes to the cadences of the King James Bible, which the young Tennessean must have heard every Sunday as a child. Classical and Biblical—the Hellenistic and Hebraic strains that Matthew Arnold identifies in *Culture and Anarchy*—are twin poles between which Ransom's expression oscillates. A third impulse that animated his poetry was Modernist, and a whiff of this may be detected in the diction of the quatrain's last line: "chattering on the air." "On" rather than "in," which we might expect.

Speaking of Ransom's classical side, the poem's message is, of course, pure carpe diem, as the third stanza makes clear:

> Practise your beauty, blue girls, before it fail;
> And I will cry with my loud lips and publish
> Beauty which all our power shall never establish,
> It is so frail.

Ever since my first reading of this poem fifty years ago, I have felt that "loud lips" violates the tone. But it is part and parcel of Ransom's ambivalent flirtation with Modernist rhetoric. "Blue Girls" was included in Ransom's book *Chills and Fever,* which

Louis Untermeyer in his introduction to Ransom in his anthology—for decades the bible of modern poetry—characterizes as "unquestionably the best volume of poetry to be published in 1924." That description not only carries, nearly seventy-five years later, a charming whiff of yesterday's literary passions; it places Ransom as a highly visible figure in the early years of literary Modernism. Ransom and Eliot shared the same birth year: 1888.

"The Love Song of J. Alfred Prufrock" had been published seven years before *Chills and Fever; The Waste Land,* not a favorite of Ransom's, was only two years old. "I have the feeling," he wrote Allen Tate in 1943, "that Waste Land is much like Picasso's Guernica, which I dislike. Also much like Dali's surrealism, which has all sorts of fine detail and no composition."

To the Biblical, the classical, and, with reservations, the Modernist, we should add a fourth focal point: the local or domestic. When I heard Ransom read "Blue Girls" in Sewanee, Tennessee, in the late 1950s, he mentioned in passing that "of course" we would know that the girls in the poem were students at the Ward Belmont School in Nashville, because of their blue uniforms. When he says, in "Lady Lost," "So I will go out into the park and say, / 'Who has lost a delicate brown-eyed lady / In the West End section?'" to readers in the wider world this would be some generic West End in some anonymous city; to readers in Middle Tennessee, he would naturally be understood to allude to the fashionable West End neighborhood in Nashville. Eliot had London, Yeats had the West of Ireland, Frost had New England, Joyce had Dublin, Faulkner had his Yoknapatawpha County: Ransom had Middle Tennessee, Nashville in particular.

While Memphis and West Tennessee had to wait until almost 1820 and Andrew Jackson's Indian Removal Act for the Chickasaws and Choctaws to sell their land to the United States and move west, thereby opening the land to white settlement, Nashville was settled in the eighteenth century by pioneers who crossed the Appalachians and claimed the rich farming country in the middle of the state. East Tennessee was a remote mountainous region, its poetry the traditional ballads brought over from the British Isles. Middle Tennessee was, and is, proud of its cultural heritage, in particular an educational tradition based on the moderate Protestantism of Methodists, Presbyterians, and Episcopalians. John Crowe Ransom's father, John James Ransom, had been a missionary to Brazil and at the time of his son's birth was a minister in the Tennessee Conference of the Methodist Church. Of the poet's grandfather, himself a minister, it was said, "No man in the Conference can equal Dick Ransom in the purity of his English." The young Ransom would have discovered his vocation among the books in his father's library.

The Middle Tennesseans of Ransom's class were farmers and professional men. "Minor gentry" might be the right term for them; they were not wealthy, they were not large landowners. They were religious and they were literate. The Methodist minister, the choir director, the lawyer, the farmer who had books in his house, the country doctor, the schoolteacher were fixtures of this society. Thomas Daniel Young, in his biography *Gentleman in a Dustcoat,* describes the future poet's summer vacations at John James Ransom's two-story brick parsonage at 337 East Main Street in Murfreesboro, Tennessee: "Ransom played tennis, visited, read, and enjoyed his mother's excellent cooking, and in the evenings the family often gathered in the parlor to hear Annie play the piano or to read together a novel by Dickens or Thackeray." A wholesome, high-minded way of life which would not be out of place in provincial, nineteenth-century England. Before television and air conditioning, some of the most important moments in Southern life were transacted on the region's broad porches and verandas on warm summer nights. As Young writes:

> On some evenings, usually when the girls were away for some reason or when Annie was busy with one of her music students, Ransom and his father would sit on the front porch and discuss religion, politics, philosophy, or literature. Often these discussions became so animated that Mrs. Ransom would caution them to hold their voices down; otherwise, she would say, the "neighbors will think you are quarreling."

The sociable, well-regulated life of the Middle Tennessee gentry is effortlessly rendered in this quatrain from "Miriam Tazewell," following a freak storm that has destroyed the garden:

The spring transpired in that year with no flowers
But the regular stars went busily on their courses,
Suppers and cards were calendared, and some bridals,
And the birds demurely sang in the bitten poplars.

After studying at Oxford as Tennessee's Rhodes Scholar, Ransom returned to this country and eventually taught at Vanderbilt University. His eminence as a professor there spawned the Tennessee branch of that flowering of literature in the South which is sometimes called the Southern Renaissance—misleadingly, because there was little in earlier Southern literary culture to be reborn. This was a birth, not a rebirth. Few professors could boast of having nurtured a better crop of students. At Vanderbilt, Allen Tate, Robert Penn Warren, Andrew Lytle, and Donald Davidson were among Ransom's students. Robert Lowell, having met Ransom through Ford Maddox Ford and Allen Tate, had gone to Nashville to study with him, then moved to Kenyon when Ransom was hired away to found the *Kenyon Review* in 1937. Randall Jarrell took a writing class from Ransom as a sophomore at Vanderbilt; when Ransom went to Kenyon, his protégé, who was by that time a graduate student, accompanied him as an English instructor and Kenyon tennis coach. The novelist Peter Taylor withdrew from Vanderbilt and followed this group of writers to Kenyon a year later.

It may have been Ransom's eminence as New Critical hierarch, literary arbiter, and editor of the most influential quarterly of its time that led readers to take his poetry for granted. Since readers of this essay may not have easy access to Ransom's poems, it may be worth mentioning that the Knopf hardcover edition of his *Selected Poems* (1991) is at this writing still in print. I'll quote one poem in its entirety, "Janet Waking," which shows how Ransom investigates a domestic scene, putting it in perspective through the use both of Biblical rhetoric and of another weapon in his rhetorical arsenal not mentioned so far in this essay: the big, Latinate word used for humorous effect. Here is "Janet Waking":

Beautifully Janet slept
Till it was deeply morning. She woke then
And thought about her dainty-feathered hen,
To see how it had kept.

One kiss she gave her mother.
Only a small one gave she to her daddy
Who would have kissed each curl of his shining baby;
No kiss at all for her brother.

"Old Chucky, old Chucky!" she cried,
Running across the world upon the grass
To Chucky's house, and listening. But alas,
Her Chucky had died.

It was a transmogrifying bee
Came droning down on Chucky's old bald head
And sat and put the poison. It scarcely bled,
But how exceedingly

And purply did the knot
Swell with the venom and communicate
Its rigor! Now the poor comb stood up straight
But Chucky did not.

So there was Janet
Kneeling on the wet grass, crying her brown hen
(Translated far beyond the daughters of men)
To rise and walk upon it.

And weeping fast as she had breath
Janet implored us, "Wake her from her sleep!"
And would not be instructed in how deep
Was the forgetful kingdom of death.


A master of rhetoric, who can play or be serious at will, is at
work here. Even beginning the first declarative sentence on the
adverb "beautifully" is evidence of the poet's mastery of syntax.
So is the grace of "Till it was deeply morning." The ABBA
stanza, enclosing two lines of pentameter within two lines of trimeter, is decorative and elegant. Unusual for Ransom, most of
the rhymes are full, with only the well-chosen inexactness of
"daddy" and "baby" lending the second stanza a rumpled inti-
macy, and the lovely "Janet" / "upon it" of the next-to-last stanza
adding to the poem's sense of amused gravity.

The second stanza runs the risk of being too mundane—an
example of where the domestic poet can run into problems
with tone. This poem, like many of Ransom's, encompasses the

domestic sphere within the larger world, as is clear when Janet runs "across the world upon the grass / To Chucky's house." Word-choice plays a major role in this encompassment, most noticeably with the "transmogrifying bee." Whether this ironic use of the humorously long Latinate word within a context of plain quotidian events owes something to T. S. Eliot's practice in his *Poems* (1920), it is hard to say. Here are two quatrains from Eliot's "Whispers of Immortality," about Grishkin; famously "Uncorseted, her friendly bust / Gives promise of pneumatic bliss":

> The sleek Brazilian jaguar
> Does not in its arboreal gloom
> Distil so rank a feline smell
> As Grishkin in a drawing-room.

> And even the Abstract Entities
> Circumambulate her charm;
> But our lot crawls between dry ribs
> To keep our metaphysics warm.

Reviewers in the early 1920s detected a resemblance between these poets, one working in a London bank, consorting with the likes of Lady Ottoline Morrell and the Sitwells, the other living in Nashville, close to home at the center of the Fugitive literary group. The *New York Times Book Review* in 1924, commenting on Ransom's book *Chills and Fever*, mentions the "sophisticated obliqueness" that made the reviewer think of Eliot. Babette Deutsch detected the influence of Eliot and Laforgue. Where Eliot is arch, dry, cosmopolitan, and sexually conflicted, Ransom is arch, dry, deliberately provincial, and very much the paterfamilias.

The irony of what Ransom accomplishes by word-choice is similar to what Faulkner does in his fiction, giving us the experience of an educated mind looking down into a simpler world. Later in the poem, the role of language in mediating between levels of experience is emphasized by the dead hen's being characterized as "Translated far beyond the daughters of men." This last phrase alludes of course to the New Testament, where Christ calls himself "the Son of Man." "Rise and walk," in the last line of the stanza, is gravely reminiscent of Christ's miracles, where the dead are called to wake and the lame to walk.

Ransom mixes Modernist with old-fashioned country rhetoric to the extent that it is hard to tell which linguistic realm "put the poison" comes from. The poem's emotional distancing, in describing how the bee sting swells "exceedingly // And purply," is extended with a bit of flatfooted humor: "Now the poor comb stood up straight / But Chucky did not." This gesture weds the sophisticated adult's disinclination to feel too deeply so small a matter as the death of a hen, with the grief a parent experiences when his child undergoes what is for her an important loss. In the second stanza, the family members appear in third-person guises. Only in the last stanza, as the poem reaches its most emotionally intense moment, do they become "us." The ending is among Ransom's most beautiful, with its ironic use of "would not be instructed" showing the pain and futility of trying to explain the mystery of death to a child. The phrasing attains added dignity through the graceful inversion, "in how deep / Was." Finally, one can only stand in awe of this poet's control of tone, witnessing the finely calibrated curve that lets him rise from "her daddy / Who would have kissed each curl of his shining baby" to the magisterial "forgetful kingdom of death."

"With a serious poet each minor poem may be a symbol of a major decision." That obiter dictum by Ransom which I quoted at the beginning of this piece might be taken as a comment on his own practice. Equally, a poem in twenty quatrains might be the microcosmic equivalent, for a "minor" poet, of the epic. Ransom wrote two such miniature epics: "Armageddon" and "Captain Carpenter."

"Armageddon" is an eighty-line narrative of the encounter, couched in terms of mock-chivalric combat, between Christ and Antichrist. The poem entertains, with the gleeful high spirits that issue from an artist engaging in pastiche with easy mastery, the dualities this philosophically minded poet was fond of. From the poem's first quatrain, the brio, the virtuoso use of rhythm, rhyme, and word-choice, tell us that we are in for a rare spectacle:

Antichrist, playing his lissome flute and merry
As was his wont, debouched upon the plain;
Then came a swirl of dust, and Christ drew rein,
Brooding upon his frugal breviary.

As strange and brilliant as the verbal surface is, the tale Ransom has to tell easily rises to the level of his poetic skills. It takes an unexpected turn when the two eternal adversaries, instead of fighting, discover a common sympathy:

Antichrist tendered a spray of rosemary
To serve his brother for a buttonhole;
Then Christ about his adversary's poll
Wrapped a dry palm that grew on Calvary.

In the poem a new concord, a state of innocence, where "the Wolf said Brother to the Lamb," comes into being. But Ransom is too seasoned an observer of human nature to suffer for long this equilibrium, this resolution of dualities. On the scene appears "a patriarch, / A godly liege of old malignant brood" who interrupts the love-feast between the two, with the result that "Christ sheds unmannerly his devil's pelf, / Takes ashes from the hearth and smears himself, / Calls for his smock and jennet as before," and takes the field of battle (to the tune, no doubt, of "Onward Christian Soldiers"):

Christ and his myrmidons, Christ at the head,
Chanted of death and glory and no complaisance;
Antichrist and the armies of malfeasance
Made songs of innocence and no bloodshed.

We all know who wins. But with an ironic twist the last, sympathetic word goes to Antichrist: "'These Armageddons!' he said; and later bled."

Ransom's better-known epic-in-miniature is "Captain Carpenter," the mock-chivalric story of an unfortunate quixotic campaigner—"I thought him Sirs an honest gentleman / Citizen husband soldier and scholar enow"—whose fate is to lose every battle he fights, parting successively with his nose and ears, getting his legs and arms broken, finally having his "sweet blue eyes" plucked out. Even after all this damage, he soldiers on:

> Captain Carpenter got up on his roan
> And sallied from the gate in hell's despite
> I heard him asking in the grimmest tone
> If any enemy yet there was to fight?

Many indignities await him at this point in his travails. Ransom narrates them all in a mock-solicitous tone in which pathos and hilarity mix in almost equal parts: "I would not knock old fellows in the dust / But there lay Captain Carpenter on his back."

The poem is, it would seem, an allegory, owing something perhaps to Spenser. Many have identified the unfortunate captain with the Confederacy. But the beauty of Ransom's fable is the way it teases us, tempting us to assign an identity to the hero-victim, but always dancing just beyond reach. Randall Jarrell's comments, in his essay "John Ransom's Poetry," are pertinent: "Some of Ransom's queer fabulous allegories are close, in form, to Kafka's. If you read 'Captain Carpenter' (or *Metamorphosis*, for that matter) to a quite uncultivated audience, it will be delighted with what happens but puzzle about what it means."

Whether he gave up poetry or whether poetry gave him up, we have no way of knowing. But during his eleven years in the art, John Crowe Ransom succeeded in accomplishing what few poets have been capable of doing. Young writers today talk about "finding a voice": I suspect that Ransom would have found that amusing. I doubt that he ever lay awake at night worrying about "voice"; yet his is one of the most distinctive in the history of poetry. More importantly, and beyond being a past master of his medium, he had a world, a culture, a point of view, and a language.

His world was the farms and small towns of his native Tennessee. Behind that geographical and cultural territory lay the whole of Western civilization; by background, education, and inclination, he was on intimate terms with most of it. Medieval European culture, rooted in Christian theology and folk myths sublimated to a code of aristocratic behavior, stirred his imagination with its images of chivalry, purity, courage, the opposition between good and evil, light and darkness. His point of view was that of a cultivated, classically trained man who never lost interest in the demotic world. His ironic detachment found, not without difficulty, a language for itself, shaped from classical literature, nineteenth-century oratory, and the Bible. The conversation between the agrarian and the classical—as American as Thomas Jefferson—was mirrored in the interplay between the Anglo-Saxon and Latinate strands of English. The final touch to this miraculous, unlikely mix was the challenge posed to his adamantly traditionalist sensibility by high Modernism.

# "How Different I Am from What They Think"

## *Elizabeth Bishop*

During most of her lifetime Elizabeth Bishop's poetry, while not exactly a secret, was known and admired primarily by an elite circle of readers, many of them writers and artists. She was, as her friend James Merrill put it, "a poet's poet's poet," whose exquisite work seemed all the more precious because, as in the case of John Crowe Ransom, there was so little of it. Spending much of her adult life abroad, she published only about a hundred poems during her lifetime—three thin books. Since her death in 1979 Bishop's work has come into its own. Her *Complete Poems* and *Collected Prose* are available in paperback. David Kalstone's *Becoming a Poet* details her friendships with her poetic mentor Marianne Moore and with Robert Lowell, her celebrated contemporary. Her poetry is widely anthologized, taught in colleges and universities everywhere.

With all but her intimate friends, Bishop preferred to play the part of a proper, upper-middle-class woman whom people called Miss Bishop. James Merrill has written of Bishop's "instinctive, modest, life-long impersonation of an ordinary woman." Apropos the Confessional poets, the most prominent of whom was Robert Lowell himself, Bishop commented acerbically, "You just wish they'd keep some of these things to themselves." Yet beneath the facade Elizabeth Bishop was the survivor of an unhappy childhood, unfortunate in love, prone to severe asthma

---

Review of *Elizabeth Bishop, Life and the Memory of It,* by Brett C. Millier (Berkeley: University of California Press, 1995). From the *New York Times Book Review.*

attacks that often forced her to sleep sitting up, fighting an often losing battle against alcoholism. "It's so funny"—Bishop wrote a friend in Brazil from one of her teaching jobs in the United States—"I go around so sedate and neat and sober (yes—absolutely) . . . everyone treats me with such respect and calls me Miss B—and every once in a while I feel a terrible laugh starting down in my chest—also a feeling of great pride because nobody knows.—And how different I am from what they think."

Born in Worcester, Massachusetts, in 1911, Bishop never really knew her father, who died when she was an infant. Her mother suffered a nervous breakdown shortly afterward, and was permanently hospitalized when her daughter was five. Young Elizabeth lived in Nova Scotia with her maternal grandparents, whom she adored, until she was six, when her father's parents abruptly took her off to Worcester "to be saved," as Bishop later wrote, "from a life of poverty and provincialism, bare feet, suet puddings . . . perhaps even from the inverted r's of my mother's family." While living as an orphan in the Bishops' tense, loveless household, the little girl developed psychosomatic ailments that would linger for the rest of her life. Besides a small inheritance, the one thing her paternal grandparents did give her was a good private education, culminating in four years at Vassar, where she performed brilliantly and made close friends.

In addition to childhood trauma and deracination, Bishop adapted slowly and ambivalently to the discovery that most of her romantic and sexual feelings were directed toward women. After a long freighter trip to South America, she met and fell in love with a remarkable, land-poor Brazilian aristocrat named Lota de Macedo Soares, who took Bishop under her wing, built her a studio on her country estate in Petrópolis, and provided her with the security that allowed Bishop to settle down, get her drinking under control, and do most of the writing for which she will be remembered. Lota Soares's death was one of many tragedies in the poet's life. "Sometimes," she wrote in her notebook, "it seems . . . as though only intelligent people are stupid enough to fall in love, & only stupid people are intelligent enough to let themselves be loved." The poignancy of that remark, worthy of Madame de Sévigné, is pure Bishop. She was an unhurried perfectionist, resolved "never to try to publish anything until I thought I'd done my best with it, no matter how many years it took—or never to publish at all."

Bishop was unconstrained by political correctness. Though her poem "Roosters" is the strongest feminist poem of our age, she refused to be included in all-women anthologies. She wanted to be judged on the basis of her art, not her gender. Her old-fashioned notions of privacy extended to a certain public guardedness about her sexuality. She described the political poetry she encountered in San Francisco in 1968 as "propaganda, or reportage of all-too-familiar events." But when she writes Robert Lowell that "I am green with envy of your kind of assurance," which makes his work seem "significant, illustrative, American, etc.," her biographer, Brett C. Millier, scolds: "It seems not to have occurred to her that Lowell's 'assurance' might have had as much to do with the privileges of gender as of family background."

Bishop discovered through poetry the clarity she seldom achieved in her life. In her masterly "At the Fishhouses" the sea is like what we imagine knowledge to be:

> dark, salt, clear, moving, utterly free,
> drawn from the cold hard mouth
> of the world, derived from the rocky breasts
> forever, flowing and drawn, and since
> our knowledge is historical, flowing and flown.

In another poem, "The Sandpiper," alongside the sea, in a humorous, oblique self-portrait, runs the eponymous bird: "His beak is focussed; he is preoccupied, / looking for something, something, something. / Poor bird, he is obsessed." Bishop asked her friend Alice Methfessel to have incised into her tombstone the last line of "The Bight," a poem she wrote for her own birthday, describing her life and work, picturing herself as a "little ocher dredge" clearing away marl from the harbor floor: "All the untidy activity continues, / awful but cheerful."

# W. H. Auden

*"Stop All the Clocks"*

A few years back I would sometimes hear W. H. Auden's poetry mentioned by friends who had seen the British film *Four Weddings and a Funeral.* An irony of our moment is that it often takes a movie or television show to bring literary works to people's attention. Shelby Foote became a household name after the PBS series on the Civil War brought his monumental three-volume history to the attention of the public; the opulent Merchant Ivory productions of *Howard's End* and *A Room with a View* stimulated interest in E. M. Forster's work; and no doubt the picture of a movie star adorning the cover of Edith Wharton's *Age of Innocence* led moviegoers to buy the book to see whether it was as good as the movie.

After September 11, 2001, there was the sense that the attacks on our country had made Americans more serious, and in that climate Auden's "September 1, 1939," with its eerie references to the "blind skyscrapers" of New York and its ominous evocations of a civilization under threat, seemed once again timely:

> Waves of anger and fear
> Circulate over the bright
> And darkened lands of the earth,
> Obsessing our private lives;
> The unmentionable odour of death
> Offends the September night.

That unmentionable odor became all too real in New York City.

---

Review of *The Hidden Law: The Poetry of W. H. Auden,* by Anthony Hecht. (Cambridge: Harvard University Press, 1993). From the *Gettysburg Review.*

It was Auden's poem "Funeral Blues: Stop All the Clocks" that lured me to *Four Weddings and a Funeral.* Hearing the poem recited in the movie reminded me how pure a lyric poet he could be. In his own time, though—particularly in his early years—Auden was commonly read as a spokesman for the Left. My aim here is to look at Auden's politics, mostly during the first part of his career—and in particular with reference to his poem "Spain 1937"—and see how Auden the political poet fits with Auden the writer of lyric poems like "Stop All the Clocks."

To observe that Auden's work has been neglected is not to say anything surprising. The adjective "neglected" might be applied to practically any poet from the past, even from the recent past. The work of even those poets whom we recognize as "major" tends to dwindle in our minds to a few entries in some anthology. When I started thinking of Auden recently I realized that only "Musée des Beaux Arts," "In Memory of W. B. Yeats," "As I walked out one evening," "In Praise of Limestone," and other anthology pieces came immediately to mind.

Certain poets have the gift and good fortune to define epochs. Pope did this for England's Augustan Age; Wordsworth, Byron, Shelley, and Keats for the Romantic period, and so on. In the twenty-first century a list of the poets read by everyone who reads even only a small amount of poetry would, in addition to Auden, include T. S. Eliot, Edna St. Vincent Millay, Robert Frost, e. e. cummings, Dylan Thomas, and more recently, Sylvia Plath. Increasingly, epoch-defining poets are expected to satisfy a political agenda—an expectation entertained with great urgency as early as the politically charged 1930s, the decade of Auden's greatest prominence.

"Take away the frills, and the argument of the prosecution is reduced to this," Auden wrote in his prose piece "The Public v. the late Mr. William Butler Yeats," written shortly before his well-known elegy on the great Anglo-Irish poet appeared: "'A great poet must give the right answers to the problems that perplex his generation. The deceased gave the wrong answers. Therefore the deceased was not a great poet.'" So goes the argument against Yeats, raised and rebutted by Auden. "Poetry in such a view," Yeats's defender goes on to say, "is the filling up of a social quiz; to pass with honours the poet must score not less than

75%." Readers' changing assessments of Auden's own poetry reflect their sense of his changing positions on the political problems that perplexed his generation. This is too bad, because Auden was a political poet only, in my view, because of the time in which he happened to live. Not surprisingly, as Auden's understanding of contemporary problems became more vexed, as his sense of remedies became more nuanced and skeptical, a portion of his readership felt let down. Auden's departure from the island of his birth in 1939 to become, if not an American, at least a New Yorker, was not popular at home during and after the War. Evelyn Waugh's satirical portraits of the characters Parsnip and Pimpernell in *Put Out More Flags* would appear to have been modeled on Auden and his companion Christopher Isherwood, who immigrated to America with him.

In retrospect, Auden's choice to leave England in 1939 seems a dubious decision. Anthony Hecht, in *The Hidden Law: The Poetry of W. H. Auden,* discusses the matter humorously: "Those who criticized Auden's departure from England must surely have known that had he remained he could have done nothing to advance the safety and welfare of the realm. And he might have positively endangered it, since his eyesight was so bad he could never have served in the armed forces, and if he had been recruited into another service such as the ambulance corps, he could easily have put lives in peril." But despite very good arguments against his remaining in England, his contemporaries were no doubt justified in suspecting him of disloyalty and lack of courage, particularly in terms of the sacrifices made by those who stayed.

In his youth Wystan Hugh Auden (1907–73) was one of the great rebel poets. "In a war or a revolution, a poet may do very well as a guerilla fighter or a spy, but it is unlikely that he will make a good regular soldier," he wrote; and indeed he saw himself as something of a spy in the heart of traditional British culture. He severely condemned Britain—and he was hardly alone in his perception—as a worn-out, incestuous society whose possibilities for renewal were frustrated by class distinctions and an entrenched capitalist economy. He was afraid that had he stayed in England he could only have served the Establishment, as did the figures evoked in the following account from the poem "A

Communist to Others" of the people who toady to "them": i.e., to the members of the British ruling class.

Here, in the early 1930s—his own twenties—Auden sketches a panoramic view of a culture where clever people, educators, and members of the professional and manufacturing classes are all mere facilitators for those at the top. I take "magic-makers" here to be priests, psychiatrists, and physicians, just as "wiseacres" can be seen as clever young men—like Auden himself—who brought intellectual sparkle to country-house drawing rooms:

> Their splendid people, their wiseacres,
> Professors, agents, magic-makers,
> > Their bankers and their brokers too,
> And ironmasters shall turn blue
> Shall fade away like morning dew
> > With club-room fossils.

Auden's England-bashing was gleeful. What is more, he adapted his revolutionary rhetoric from traditional models: "There is something undisguisedly good-natured about this detestation," Hecht says, "borrowed in all likelihood from the skillful invectives of the Latin poets, if not from Ronsard and the Pleiades or Skelton or Robert Burns."

Part of the genius of Auden's poetic method was that he could use traditional forms to project new perceptions. It may be true, as Edward Mendelson puts it in the preface to his 1979 edition of the *Selected Poems,* that "Auden was the first poet writing in English who felt at home in the twentieth century." At the same time he was a master of European poetic tradition, and the greatest metricist since Pope. "Anglo-Saxon and Middle English poetry have been one of my strongest, most lasting influences," Auden told an interviewer. He was lucky enough to attend lectures at Oxford by Professor J. R. R. Tolkien, who was thirty-four at the time: "I do not remember a single word he said but at a certain point he recited, and magnificently, a long passage of *Beowulf.* I was spellbound. This poetry, I knew, was going to be my dish." Auden's free version of the Anglo-Saxon heroic poem "The Seafarer," beginning "Doom is dark and deeper than any sea-dingle," shows the use he made of Anglo-Saxon, with its strong-stress alliterative line and pared-down syntax that high-lights a simple, powerful vocabulary:

> There head falls forward, fatigued at evening,
> And dreams of home,
> Waving from window, spread of welcome,
> Kissing of wife under single sheet;
> But waking sees
> Bird-flocks nameless to him, through doorway voices
> Of new men making another love.

The suggestion of a threatening kind of homosexuality is not present in the Anglo-Saxon original, but it fits the tone of the poem. In speaking of his use of Icelandic sagas and early Irish poetry, Auden implicitly acknowledges his tactic of taking a traditional meter and adapting it to his own purposes: "In general the further away from you in time or feeling that poets are, the more you can get out of them for your own use. Often some piece of technique thus learnt really unchains one's own Daimon quite suddenly."

One can see how successfully he takes the Anglo-Saxon lament—which typically tells the story of an exile who must "tread the paths of exile"—and makes it a very modern parable of what he would later call "the Age of Anxiety":

> Save him from hostile capture,
> From sudden tiger's spring at corner;
> Protect his house,
> His anxious house where days are counted
> From thunderbolt protect,
> From gradual ruin spreading like a stain;
> Converting number from vague to certain . . .

The ominous "gradual ruin spreading like a stain" suggests not the simpler world of the *comitatus,* that body of warriors attached to a chieftain or petty king, out of which most Anglo-Saxon poetry was written, so much as the end-of-empire malaise of Britain in the 1930s. In another of Auden's well-known projections of existential anxiety, "As I walked out one evening," he chose a modified ballad stanza, using a trimeter quatrain rather than the usual alternation of four- and three-beat lines. The diction is sophisticated and, in places, surrealistic. After a stylized lover makes an exaggerated claim for the strength of his affections—"I'll love you, dear, I'll love you / Till China and Africa meet"—whirring and chiming clocks rebut his assertions:

> "In headaches and in worry
> Vaguely life leaks away,
> And Time will have his fancy
> To-morrow or to-day.
>
> "Into many a green valley
> Drifts the appalling snow;
> Time breaks the threaded dances
> And the diver's brilliant bow.
>
> "O plunge your hands in water,
> Plunge them in up to the wrist;
> Stare, stare in the basin
> And wonder what you've missed.
>
> "The glacier knocks in the cupboard,
> The desert sighs in the bed,
> And the crack in the tea-cup opens
> A lane to the land of the dead."

As Auden was to discover by the late 1930s, it is easier to identify the stench of corruption than to introduce the cleanly fragrance of health. The precocious young Oxford man's acute satires suggested that violent revolution would clear away the debris of the past and usher in the new order. Given a jaunty rhythm by his trademark use of what Hecht identifies as his "rollicking amphibrachs" ( / * * / ), Auden's revolutionary verses would look crashingly unsound only a few years later—not to mention the ironic spin put on them today by the worldwide collapse of Communism and the new air of sobriety in a world where terrorism has become the order of the day.

> It's farewell to the drawing-room's civilised cry,
> The professor's sensible whereto and why,
> The frock-coated diplomat's social aplomb,
> Now matters are settled with gas and with bomb.

It is clear now that proletarian revolution followed by military dictatorship did not settle matters but simply, as we have seen in Eastern Europe and the former Soviet Union, put historical conflicts into a deep sleep from which they would eventually wake, with bloodthirsty populations bent on redressing old wrongs. Auden was, of course, a romantic revolutionary, as is clear from poems like "Spain 1937," which contains stanzas (later to be revised and rendered equivocal) like

> To-day the deliberate increase in the chances of death,
> The conscious acceptance of guilt in the necessary murder;
> To-day the expending of powers
> On the flat ephemeral pamphlet and the boring meeting.

> To-day the makeshift consolations: the shared cigarette,
> The cards in the candlelit barn, and the scraping concert,
> The masculine jokes; to-day the
> Fumbled and unsatisfactory embrace before hurting.

That Auden should have gained notoriety in Britain because of poems like "Spain" is ironic, since Spain broke the back of his own belief in the coming of the socialist millennium. The artist Sir William Coldstream writes:

> He was at this time much more taken up with political ideas than formerly, though I do not think he ever had any real appetite for politics. It was, I think, curiosity as well as social conscience that made him go to Spain in the civil war. I remember seeing him off at the station. After he came back, it was my impression that his Spanish experience had slightly shaken his faith in revolutionary solutions.

In his essay "Inside the Whale," George Orwell, who in Spain had had his own eyes opened to the frequent dishonesty of agitprop and the brutality of guerilla warfare, famously called Auden's poem

> a sort of thumb-nail sketch of a day in the life of a "good party man." In the morning a couple of political murders, a ten minutes' interlude to stifle "bourgeois" remorse, then a hurried luncheon and a busy afternoon and evening chalking

walls and distributing pamphlets . . . The Hitlers and Stalins find murder necessary, but they don't advertise their callousness, and they don't speak of it as murder; it is "liquidation," "elimination," some other soothing phrase. Mr. Auden's brand of amoralism is only possible if you are the kind of person who is always somewhere else when the trigger is pulled.

Perhaps Auden's honesty, which prevented him from calling murder anything other than murder, was what led him—sooner rather than later—to abandon Marxism. Orwell extends his critique of the language of totalitarianism in his influential essay "Politics and the English Language," which is must-reading for anyone with a serious interest in how language gets manipulated in ideological closed systems. Anthony Hecht is hardly less severe on Auden:

> Generally speaking, this notion of comradely feeling rising up suddenly into a "people's army" [see the second stanza quoted above] has all the daydream laxity I associate with left-wing, dirty-footed bohemians in Greenwich Village lofts, joining in singing the popular loyalist songs to the accompaniment of somebody's semi-skilled guitar music, and passing the Gallo jug . . . Fighting a war is not joining a brotherhood of like-minded friends, and "hours of friendship" do not make a fighting force. It is the sheer unreality of these details of a poem that so fiercely desires to insist upon reality that makes such passages completely unpersuasive.

"Semi-skilled" is delicious. The scene sketched here will be familiar to many people, even if for Greenwich Village you read Berkeley or Madison or Evanston, and for "Gallo jug" you read "joint." It is not hard to picture Bob Dylan or Allen Ginsberg in the company Hecht describes. Those of us who were infatuated with the idea of revolutionary violence as recently as thirty years ago will sympathize with the attraction it held for Auden and his generation. A retrospective, printed in his invaluable prose collection, *The Dyer's Hand,* on the poetry that made him the spokesman for a revolutionary generation is shrewd and complex:

> The work of a young writer . . . is sometimes a therapeutic act. He finds himself obsessed by certain ways of feeling and thinking of which his instinct tells him he must be rid before he can discover his authentic interests and sympathies, and the only way by which he can be rid of them forever is by surrendering to them. Once he has done this, he has developed the necessary antibodies which will make him immune for the rest of his life. As a rule, the disease is some spiritual malaise of his generation. If so, he may, as Goethe did, find himself in an embarrassing situation. What he wrote in order to exorcise certain feelings is enthusiastically welcomed by his contemporaries because it expresses just what they feel but, unlike him, they are perfectly happy to feel in this way; for the moment they regard him as their spokesman. Time passes. Having gotten the poison out of his system, the writer turns to his true interests which are not, and never were, those of his early admirers, who now pursue him with cries of "Traitor!"

Later in life, as Hecht correctly points out, Auden would criticize utopian thinking of the kind expressed in "Spain," pointing out that "the forward-looking Utopian . . . necessarily believes that his New Jerusalem is a dream that ought to be realized so that the actions by which it could be realized are a necessary element in his dream . . ." In a letter to Monroe K. Spears, an early and incisive commentator on his poetry (see Spears's book *The Poetry of W. H. Auden: The Disenchanted Island* [1963]), he directly answered critics of his stance in "Spain":

> I was not excusing totalitarian crimes but only trying to say what, surely, every decent person thinks if he finds himself unable to adopt the absolute pacifist position. (1) To kill another human being is always murder and should never be called anything else. (2) In a war, the members of two rival groups try to murder their opponents. (3) If there is such a thing as a just war, then murder can be necessary for the sake of "justice."

Even if we grant that Auden was naive and that his naivete temporarily led him to acquiesce in the brutality of revolutionary violence, still his romantic vision of the future represents, for me, utopian dreaming at its loveliest:

To-morrow, perhaps the future. The research on fatigue
And the movements of packers; the gradual exploration of
    all the
        Octaves of radiation;
To-morrow the enlarging of consciousness by diet and
    breathing.

To-morrow the rediscovery of romantic love,
The photographing of ravens; all the fun under
        Liberty's masterful shadow;
To-morrow the hour of the pageant-master and the
    musician,

The beautiful roar of the chorus under the dome,
To-morrow the exchanging of tips on the breeding of
    terriers,
        The eager election of chairmen
By the sudden forest of hands. But today the struggle.

Tomorrow for the young the poets exploding like bombs,
The walks by the lake, the weeks of perfect communion;
        To-morrow the bicycle races
Through the suburbs on summer evenings. But today the
    struggle.

Hecht supplies a historical coda to these lines by quoting
lines from Joseph Brodsky's poem "Lagoon" that echo this part
of "Spain"—"either consciously or unconsciously" according to
Hecht. Brodsky, who of course had to live under real rather
than utopian Marxism, writes of "that nation where among /
Forests of hands the tyrant of the State / Is voted in, its only
candidate."

While in his later years Auden may have grown in wisdom—
becoming the Saint Wystan of many of the memoirs collected in
Stephen Spender's splendid memorial volume, *W. H. Auden: A
Tribute,* and of James Merrill's *Changing Light at Sandover*—his
poetry did desiccate and lose its youthful, thrilling imperti-
nence. At the same time, though, that he was making the classic
journey from undergraduate socialist to sexagenarian Tory,
Auden's verse never lost its authority. (A good and inexpensive
source in which to follow the unfolding of Auden's gift is Ed-

ward Mendelson's 1979 paperback edition of the *Selected Poems,* which reprints the poems chronologically, in the form of their first book publications.) His biographers describe him as working fast and decisively when he wrote; the clarity of his rhetoric rings clear as a silver dollar. Regarded as a personality, Auden may be in fact more attractive as the ageing High Anglican martini-drinking aphorist with a face (to quote its owner) "like a wedding-cake left out in the rain," who wore carpet slippers and a grease-spattered dinner jacket to the opera, than as the precocious but wet-behind-the-ears pamphleteer with an interest in revolution and psychoanalysis. But I can't pretend that his later work rivals the verve of early pieces like "Doom is dark and deeper than any sea-dingle," "Consider this and in our time," "Voltaire at Ferney," and a dozen or two more.

Paramount in Auden's life work are three main ideas. These are language, the idea of the hero, and a belief in the frivolity of art. I will take them up, digressively, in reverse order. The last of the three emphases may be seen as Auden's allegiance to something resembling a camp aesthetic. Of Yeats he wrote approvingly: "You were silly like us." He often remarked that a love for the high-camp opera *Norma* was his true test of a person's good taste. In "Vespers," from *The Shield of Achilles,* the poet comments archly: "In my Eden a person who dislikes Bellini has the good manners not to get born . . ." Typical of Hecht's urbane manner is his gloss on this statement: "It is necessary first to explain that the Bellini mentioned is not, alas, one of the great family of Venetian painters, but instead Vincenzo Bellini, composer of *Norma* and *I Puritani.* There is, admittedly, no way for the uninstructed reader to figure this out; one simply has to be acquainted with Auden's particular tastes, which in the course of time he elevated into 'tests' by which he rather arbitrarily determined who was civilized."

An understanding of the role of camp as a way of putting a brave face on the unendurable—particularly when one considers it as a distinctive feature of gay sensibility—helps explain how movingly the lyric "Funeral Blues: Stop All the Clocks" comes across as read in *Four Weddings and a Funeral* by John Hannah, who plays the role of Matthew. Here is the poem:

Stop all the clocks, cut off the telephone,
Prevent the dog from barking with a juicy bone,
Silence the pianos and with muffled drum
Bring out the coffin, let the mourners come.

Let aeroplanes circle moaning overhead
Scribbling on the sky the message He Is Dead,
Put crepe bows round the white necks of the public doves,
Let the traffic policemen wear black cotton gloves.

He was my North, my South, my East and West,
My working week and my Sunday rest,
My noon, my midnight, my talk, my song;
I thought that love would last for ever: I was wrong.

The stars are not wanted now; put out every one:
Pack up the moon and dismantle the sun;
Pour away the ocean and sweep up the woods:
For nothing now can ever come to any good.

Matthew reads this poem at the funeral of his companion, Gareth, played by Simon Callow, whose splendid waistcoats and exuberant manner are matched by the seemingly inappropriate elements of this poem, which Matthew introduces as "the words of another splendid bugger, W. H. Auden." At many another funeral, "crepe bows round the white necks of the public doves," black gloves on the hands of policemen, the "moaning" aeroplanes of skywriters, etc., would not seem in keeping with the solemnity of the occasion. The frivolity of these images, and the speaker's brave determination to be "toujours gay," create an unforgettable poetic as well as cinematic moment. I call this poem a lyric, though it is more obviously an elegy, because while the emotions are personal, our impressions of the man who has died are not narrowly specific.

Auden's stated belief in the non-essentiality of art ties in with both his early identification with revolutionary politics—where only "the struggle" is important—and his late return to Christianity, when he wrote: "From the Christian point of view and in spite of all aesthetics, any poet's existence is a sin, viz., the sin that one is writing poetry instead of living; that one occupies oneself with God and truth only in one's imagination instead of aiming at experiencing both existentially."

To address the second of the topics, the hero was a shifting but vitally important figure. At one point he was Lenin, or again D. H. Lawrence—at another point Freud. For Auden, the son of a physician, these figures often represented "healers," whom he often romanticized, as when he says of Freud that "To us he is no more a person / Now but a whole climate of opinion."

> He extends, till the tired in even
> The remotest most miserable duchy
> Have felt the change in their bones and are cheered,
> And the child unlucky in his little State,
> Some hearth where freedom is excluded,
> A hive whose honey is fear and worry,
> Feels calmer now and somehow assured of escape.

And yet perhaps Auden's enthusiasm for Freud stretches credulity. Anthony Hecht writes, "This strikes me as among the feebler and more sentimental claims the poem makes. In a world in which child abuse is rampant, there cannot be many 'unlucky' children who are for a moment calmed and soothed by the fact that Freud lived, or that, in parts of society that have nothing to do with such children, his ideas are honored and his methods put into practice." That we have few authentic heroes in our time made Auden's search for them all the more problematic.

Auden's commitment to language was his most absolute value. In *The Dyer's Hand* he defined the qualities that would help one identify promise in a young writer: "'Why do you want to write poetry?' If the young man answers: 'I have important things I want to say,' then he is not a poet. If he answers: 'I like hanging around words listening to what they say,' then maybe he is going to be a poet." In a letter to his cousin Anne Fremantle, he asserted: "The duties of a writer as a writer and a citizen are not the same. The only duty a writer has as a citizen is to defend language. And this is a political duty. Because if language is corrupted, thought is corrupted."

Auden searched through various avenues for the hidden secret, the obscured synthesis that would infuse freedom with responsibility, duty with joy. This search partly explains his fascination with detective stories, so delightfully expounded in his essay "The Guilty Vicarage." The presence of a mystery and the necessity of solving it, as an existential metaphor, plays itself out in his "New Year Letter" of 1941:

> The situation of our time
> Surrounds us like a baffling crime.
> There lies the body half-undressed,
> We all had reason to detest,
> And all are suspects and involved
> Until the mystery is solved.

No wonder, then, that while two of Auden's heroes were the detective and the spy, another was the scientific "investigator" who "peers through his instruments / At the inhuman provinces, the virile bacillus / Or enormous Jupiter finished." Christopher Isherwood, in his 1937 piece "Some Notes on Auden's Early Poetry," states that

Auden is essentially a scientist: perhaps I should add, "a schoolboy scientist." He has, that is to say, the scientific training and the scientific interests of a very intelligent schoolboy. He has covered the groundwork, but doesn't propose to go any further: he has no intention of specializing. Nevertheless, he has acquired the scientific outlook and technique of approach; and this is really all he needs for his writing.

Early and late, Auden's answers to the problems that perplexed his generation were not always, in retrospect, the right ones. But if he was carried away by a naively romantic version of Marxism, so were many of his European and American contemporaries. If Freud has turned out to be a more equivocal hero than he seemed in 1939, certainly he was a better choice than Pound's hero, Mussolini. And if Auden's journey back to the Anglican church is not one on which every reader would accompany him, still his version of Christianity seems less forbidding, more forgiving of human weakness than that of his coreligionist T. S. Eliot. In the end it is Auden's intelligence, his lack of cant, his sincere determination to ask the pertinent questions, that make his poetry of permanent interest.

# Digging for the Truth about
# Sylvia Plath

As every reader of modern poetry knows, on February 11, 1963, Sylvia Plath took her own life, turning on the gas oven in her flat at 23 Fitzroy Road, London, and laying her head inside on a folded cloth. The poems she wrote during the last two years of her life have become the stuff of legend. For decades now, discussions of Plath's poetry, her life, and the implications of both for literature, for the relations between women and men, for questions of literary ownership—and every other tangent and tangential subject—have flowed fast and furiously. The jaundiced eye would see this as "the Plath industry": there have been, as Lucas Myers puts it in a memoir appended to Anne Stevenson's *Bitter Fame*, "a lot of people prepar[ed] to board the Sylvia train, some of them with small baggage of scruple." It is also genuinely true that, as Jacqueline Rose writes in *The Haunting of Sylvia Plath*, people are drawn to Plath's story because it illuminates many vexed questions in our culture. As a result of all the attention paid to her, we know more about Plath than we did when *Ariel* forced its way, seemingly out of nowhere, into our consciousness, with a power that demanded full attention.

Here, rather than giving an interpretation of her poetry, I shall focus on her life and the uses commentators have made of it. Of the commentators I examine here, Paul Alexander sets

Review of *Bitter Fame*, by Anne Stevenson (New York: Houghton Mifflin, 1990); *Rough Magic*, by Paul Alexander (New York: Viking, 1991); *The Haunting of Sylvia Plath*, by Jacqueline Rose (Cambridge: Harvard University Press, 1992); and *Crow Steered Bergs Appeared: A Memoir of Ted Hughes and Sylvia Plath*, by Lucas Myers (Sewanee, Tenn.: Proctor's Hall Press, 2001). From the *Gettysburg Review*.

out to tell a sensationalized story, perhaps with a movie contract in mind, while for Jacqueline Rose, Plath's life is fodder for cultural criticism, and if the details don't fit, they can be fudged. Lucas Myers, a close friend to Hughes and Plath, turns up often as a biographical source. While Anne Stevenson tries to tell the story fairly, using Myers as one of her sources, the frustrations she encounters may only prove the impossibility of not being pilloried by one side or the other in this highly disputed territory.

Plath was all writer. It wasn't that she always "knew she wanted to be a writer," as people will say of themselves or others—but that from her very earliest days she was engaged with language and literature. Before her third birthday she had taught herself to read capital letters from signboards and was encouraged by her mother, Aurelia, to pick out letters from the newspaper to keep herself busy while her mother was occupied with her younger brother. Anne Stevenson makes the point that "what Mrs. Plath does not say—a fact surely relevant to Sylvia's recourse to language in times of difficulty—is that even at two and a half her daughter was being urged to treat negative emotion (jealousy of her brother) with words." From Scout camp she writes that the ill-bred language of other children "just hurts my ears. I long for my family's soft sweet talk."

Aurelia Plath records that Sylvia wrote her family 696 letters between 1950 and her death in 1963—roughly one letter a week. What remains of the journals she kept beginning in childhood would amount to about one thousand printed pages. This does not include two volumes covering the crucial period from 1959 to her death—one of which Ted Hughes says he destroyed, one of which he reports as having "disappeared." The ethics of his destroying the one notebook—"because I did not want her children to have to read it"—have been the subject of much debate. His action is hard to defend. Rumor has it, incidentally, that both notebooks still exist. In addition to the letters and journals, there are Plath's novel *The Bell Jar,* plus *Johnny Panic and the Bible of Dreams and Other Prose Writings,* not to mention her poetry, almost all of which is available in her *Collected Poems.* For someone who died at thirty, Sylvia Plath was stupendously prolific.

Her own writings—both literary and personal—and the writings about her introduce one into the much-disputed puzzle of her life, her labyrinthine personality and complex set of personal myths. Any reader motivated to know all there is to know about Sylvia Plath must master a daunting amount of material. This is how Dido Merwin sums it up in her memoir of Plath—colorfully and crisply written, but dripping with venom—which is appended to *Bitter Fame:*

> It was essential to possess all three keys to her labyrinth before one could make head or tail of a number of things that, at the time, were totally incomprehensible. In all, it took about twenty years: in '65 the Ariel poems disclosed the consuming hatred and fury, the implications of which none of her self-styled biographers, so far as I know, have ever had the objectivity and guts to face up to. In '75, the gospel according to the Desired Image—*Letters Home*—appeared, introducing us to a highly organized mythologising that turned everything to favour and to prettiness. Finally, in '82, the Journals revealed Sylvia's personal Armageddon: the struggles between what Ted in his foreword called "her warring selves." It also confirmed that the name of her Dybbuk was Fear.

It is hard not to feel that two selves inhabited Sylvia Plath: one of them the hurt self, traumatized and grieving, that hid underground in reaction to the pain of her father's death—"that troubled, vital, inaccessible part of her," as Stevenson puts it, "touched on in her best poems and darkly expressed in her journals. Plath's true subject was this inner self, not her outer experiences and achievements. Eventually she would yearn to kill her false self so that her real one might burn free of it." The other self was the straight-A scholarship student, who wrote her mother from Smith: "You are listening to the most busy and happy girl in the world . . . Honestly, Mum, I could just cry with happiness. I love this place so, and there is so much to do creatively . . . The world is splitting open at my feet like a ripe, juicy watermelon. If only I can work, work, work to justify all my opportunities. Your happy girl, Sivvy."

It's easy to sneer at this kind of gush, and there's too much condescension in *Bitter Fame,* whether it comes from Ted Hughes's sister Olwyn's emendations or from Anne Stevenson's complaisance in the English intellectual's envy-tinged habit of putdown. Note the use of the word "American" here: "Some of her friends speak warmly of her charm, her humor, her great gifts and huge capacity for affection," the preface tells us. "Others recall a complex, completely self-absorbed, stubbornly ambitious American whose outer shell of bright capability contained a seething core of inexplicable fury." After her marriage to Ted Hughes, we are told, "Mrs. Sylvia Hughes was indeed quite a different person from the garish, sexually rapacious man-chaser of her first terms." This brand of maliciousness (I suspect the hand of Olwyn Hughes) belongs more in a poison-pen letter than in a work of literary criticism.

Still, being a brilliant, impecunious over-achiever among the daughters of the rich at Smith put a strain on Plath that would prove unbearable:

> To go to college fraternity parties where a boy buries his face in your neck or tries to rape you if he isn't satisfied with burying his fingers in the flesh of your breast. To learn that there are a million girls who are beautiful and that each day more leave behind the awkward teenage stage, as you once did, and embark on the adventure of being loved and petted. To be aware that you must compete somehow, and yet that wealth and beauty are not in your realm. To learn that a boy will make a careless remark about "your side of town" as he drives you to a roadhouse in his father's latest chromium-plated convertible. To learn that you might have been more of an artist than you are if you had been born into a family of wealthy intellectuals . . .

As early as her college years Plath began to feel the need to purge her false self: "The purging usually took the form of a serious risk. Once the risk was taken and overcome, balance was restored and guilt banished, its occasion no longer of importance." Her college roommate comments that it was "almost as though only being snatched from the brink of death could she confirm her worth."

The first symbolic death and resurrection we know of (the "accident" at age ten referred to in "Lady Lazarus" remains a mystery) occurred in 1952, re-created retrospectively in *The Bell Jar:*

> I plummeted down past the zigzaggers, the students, the experts, through year after year of doubleness and smiles and compromises, into my own past.
>
> People and trees receded on either hand like the dark sides of a tunnel as I hurtled on to the still, bright point at the end of it, the pebble at the bottom of the well, the white sweet baby cradled in its mother's belly.

The second was her honest-to-God suicide attempt in 1953, which followed her stint in New York City as a guest editor of *Mademoiselle* magazine, Frank O'Connor's rejection of her application to be a student in his story-writing class at Harvard Summer School, and the electroconvulsive (shock) therapy the family doctor, Francesca Racioppi, had prescribed for her. That she recovered from two days of unconsciousness brought on by swallowing forty sleeping pills may have cemented in Plath's mind the notion that she had become an expert in the death-and-rebirth game. Confidence in her ultimate resurrection gives "Lady Lazarus" its bravado:

> The first time it happened I was ten.
> It was an accident.
>
> The second time I meant
> To last it out and not come back at all.
> I rocked shut
>
> As a seashell.
> They had to call and call
> And pick the worms off me like sticky pearls.
>
> Dying
> is an art, like everything else.
> I do it exceptionally well.
>
> I do it so it feels like hell.
> I do it so it feels real.
> I guess you could say I've a call.

It's easy enough to do it in a cell.
It's easy enough to do it and stay put.
It's the theatrical

Comeback in broad day
To the same place, the same face, the same brute
Amused shout:

"A miracle!"
That knocks me out.

The double tragedy of this suicide attempt was (1) that it planted in her mind the idea she had attained mastery over death and (2) that her psychiatrist, Dr. Ruth Beuscher, prescribed shock treatment to bring her out of the state she was in. In her condition she could not read or write, she could not even tell one letter from another—the most extreme disorientation imaginable for a person whose very life was the written word. Olive Prouty, the wealthy novelist who helped send Sylvia Plath to Smith and who befriended her in many other ways, accused Dr. J. Peter Thornton, who had administered shock treatment before the suicide attempt, of having driven her to suicide: "I think her attempt at suicide was due largely to the horror of what she remembers of the shock treatments, and the fears aroused." And Anne Stevenson writes: "Certainly the experience of shock treatment during her prolonged summer breakdown and again during the purgatory of her 'cure' affected Sylvia more deeply than anyone understood at the time. It may be that she never really recovered from it, that it changed her personality permanently, stripping her of a psychological 'skin' she could ill afford to lose. Attributable to her ECT is the unseen menace that haunts nearly everything she wrote, her conviction that the world, however benign in appearance, conceals dangerous animosity, directed particularly toward herself."

*Bitter Fame* is the best book written on Plath so far—at least parts of it are. The book was celebrated though controversial in Britain, where the literary community, smaller and more interconnected than in the U.S., had a sense of the dynamics that went into its making. Here, where the book has not sold well, it is generally dismissed, by people who have not read it, as "the authorized biography"—the Hughes family's version of the story. Helen Vendler, always one of the most reliable commentators on contemporary poetry, wrote a convincingly damaging review of the book in the *New Republic* (November 1989). Still, having sensed something of the "divided" nature of the project, I wrote Anne Stevenson, the American-born poet—resident in England for many years—and author of one of the first book-length studies of Elizabeth Bishop, and queried her about *Bitter Fame*. She kindly replied in detail on July 20, 1992, giving me permission to quote her. "Looking back on it," she writes, "it seems clear that I wanted to write one kind of book, Olwyn another."

For readers unfamiliar with these disputes: Olwyn, Ted Hughes's sister, is a literary agent who has had much to do with the disposition of her sister-in-law's literary estate. It seems fair to say that she and Sylvia Plath loathed one another. "You liked her," Paul Alexander quotes a London newspaper's account of Olwyn's comment to Clarissa Roche, a friend of Sylvia Plath's, "I think she was pretty straight poison. God preserve me from mixed-up kids." In exchange for permission to quote from Sylvia Plath's writings, Olwyn Hughes has demanded editorial control over the works in which the quotations appear. To avoid having their work vetted by the Plath estate, Paul Alexander and Jacqueline Rose limited their direct quotations. Earlier, in the preface to her 1986 biography of Plath, Linda Wagner Martin reported: "Olwyn wrote me at great length, usually in argument with my views about the life and development of Plath. Ted Hughes responded to a reading of the manuscript in draft form in 1986 with suggestions for changes that filled fifteen pages and would have meant a deletion of more than 15,000 words."

Stevenson found herself in a dilemma. Olwyn was instrumental in bringing to light certain sources—"people who knew Sylvia and Ted well as a couple and hadn't wanted to embarrass Ted by taking part in the Plath fray while his children were growing up"—that might not have been accessible to Stevenson working on her own. "It became obvious to me, quite early on, that Olwyn and Dido [Merwin] had worked themselves into a rage about feminist and other misrepresentations of Sylvia's puzzling, divided character during the 60s and 70s when Plath's poetry geysered into fame . . . I had always seen Plath as a literary phenomenon, not a literary genius, and here was an opportunity to show how her protected American background, her gifts, her paranoia, idealism, susceptibility to psychological theory, extreme ambition and excited marriage to England's most promising and daring young poet of the 1950s all fell into a pattern typical of young college-educated American women of the time."

At first Olwyn Hughes simply provided material and offered comments on what Stevenson had written. "Finally, though, instead of sending comments, Olwyn herself began to draft large sections she insisted had to go into the book . . . I began to see that I had weighed down the book too much with Olwyn's evidence." The poet Peter Davison, the book's editor at Houghton Mifflin, trying to reconcile the opposing camps, "did, after all, diplomatically produce a text that I could call mostly mine and Olwyn could pride herself on calling partly hers. That is the state of the book today. The introduction and the first ten chapters are much as I wrote them over Christmas and New Year, 1987–88. Olwyn insisted on adding paragraphs about a dressing gown and other minor matters; I think you can tell when her voice intrudes . . . I wish now I had not agreed to publish the last chapters in their present form, but in 1989 I was dead exhausted after fighting . . . I don't think, with Olwyn, that she was fundamentally 'mad' or 'psychotic,' though she was certainly an hysteric, and it is possible she had acute premenstrual syndrome, which would explain her extreme manic-depressiveness. I feel very sorry for her—as my poem, 'Letter to Sylvia Plath' suggests." She concludes, "Probably I shouldn't have agreed to publish *Bitter Fame* . . ."

But I am glad she did. With all the editorial compromises, one might ask, why do I maintain this is the best book to have been written on Plath? First, because Stevenson is the most insightful reader of poetry to have undertaken a book-length study of Plath's work. Second, because Stevenson is a contemporary of Sylvia Plath's, with an insider's feeling for American society during the 1950s, particularly for the life of a brilliant female college student of that era. Third, the testimonies of many people who knew Plath and Hughes place the poet more firmly in the surround of her life and times than has been done before. There are many details here not available elsewhere. The description of Sylvia Plath in London the winter she died, having spent a birthday check from Olive Prouty on new clothes— "a camel suit and matching sweater, a black sweater and blue tweed skirt, a green cardigan and red skirt . . . With a new hair style and black leather bag, gloves, and shoes, she was going to take London by storm"—is juxtaposed with a description of the cut thumb she had written about in "Cut," the poem that begins "What a thrill— / My thumb instead of an onion"—"bound up in a dirty bandage . . . clearly septic and in need of attention." A heartbreaking image of Sylvia Plath, inner and outer. Read *Bitter Fame* critically, but by all means read it.

Anne Stevenson, though sympathetic toward Plath, has no truck with what Linda Wagner Martin has called "the Plath legend," with its picture of her as a passive sufferer of ill treatment from a demonized Ted Hughes. Sylvia Plath was an exceptionally persuasive rhetorician and myth-maker—talents that seem, because of their very effectiveness, to have escaped the attention of those who have made Plath into a feminist martyr. After all, doesn't the poem "Daddy" say that Sylvia Plath's father was a Nazi and a sadist?

> I have always been scared of you,
> With your Luftwaffe, your gobbledygoo.
> And your neat moustache
> And your Aryan eye, bright blue.
> Panzer-man, panzer-man, O You—
>
> Not God but a swastika
> So black no sky could squeak through.
> Every woman adores a Fascist,
> The boot in the face, the brute
> Brute heart of a brute like you.

For college sophomores to take this literally is understandable. The willingness of other readers to ignore signs that the "brute" here is part fictional character, part projection of the author's own internal violence, is as much a tribute to the power of Plath's rhetoric as it is to the willingness of feminists to believe they had found poetry that could be used as a case study of the things that had always said about men. There's no evidence to suggest that Otto Plath was anything other than an old-fashioned German paterfamilias.

For readers who hold to the notion of Sylvia Plath as the wronged party in a marital melodrama, in which Ted Hughes plays a dark, even Satanic role, Paul Alexander's *Rough Magic* is the book to read. It is less a biography than a kind of gothic romance in which Plath's subjective readings of events—particularly those fueled by hatred toward Ted Hughes immediately after the couple separated in 1962—are treated as fact. Too bad the entire book is not as attractively written as the opening, which evokes the atmosphere of a good romance:

> The landscape surrounding the country house in Devon lay dead, silent—typical for this hour of the early morning . . . In one upstairs bedroom, two small children, a girl not yet three and an infant boy ten months old, slept peacefully in their beds. Down the hall, in a room converted into a study, a young woman, the house's only other inhabitant, hunched at her desk. Her frame was thin—for several months she had been steadily losing weight—and her face was chalky and pale. Her long brown fall of hair hung down tangled and unkempt . . .

Alexander's credibility as a biographer of Plath—most of whose adult life was lived in England—is enhanced if one hasn't traveled outside the United States much. He refers to the well-known Sainte-Chapelle in Paris as "the Seine Chapel," for example, and sees Britain as a benighted medieval land whose inhabitants adhere to strange occult practices and haven't been enlightened by American plumbing. Here we have Ted Hughes's mother: "Not unlike many inhabitants of Yorkshire, an isolated region in which the average citizen frowned on progress and clung to religion and superstition, Edith, it was rumored, studied magic, passing her knowledge on to her children. Finally, this explained Ted's avid interest in horoscopes, hypnosis, and mind control." A little research into the bohemian literary milieu that Hughes and his friends moved in would reveal a widespread and largely harmless interest in the occult. In literary Paris and London in the late 1950s astrology, Tarot cards, etc., enjoyed just as much of a vogue as they did near the corner of Haight and Ashbury in the 1960s. Much of that atmosphere can be gleaned from Lucas Myers's *Crow Steered Bergs Appeared,* which deserves to be better known.

With his obsession with state-of-the-art plumbing Paul Alexander comes across as a stereotypical American tourist scandalized by the bathing facilities of European hotels. Here's what he says about the private bath the Hugheses paid extra for in their honeymoon hotel: "The tub was a luxury for Ted, who, growing up in Yorkshire, had never before had regular access to such private facilities. He became so overjoyed as he took his shower each day that Sylvia could hear him squawking riotously in the tub. But Sylvia did not complain. These were the first baths Ted had taken since the morning of their wedding."

Identifying one-sidedly with Plath's own views of people and events, the biographer tells us: "Since Ted's mother, Edith, in Sylvia's eyes, did little to help around the house (Sylvia described her to Aurelia as a lazy woman who lay in bed until noon), Sylvia had to assume the burden of cooking and cleaning not only for her family but for her guests." This description of her mother-in-law does not appear in *Letters Home,* though the tactful Aurelia Plath may well have edited it out. But would it not, in the interests of ordinary decency, have been appropriate to mention that Edith Hughes suffered from crippling arthritis, which may have prevented her from rising before noon? Alexander is entitled to his loathing for Ted Hughes, but why bash his deceased mother?

Though it's hard to guess what Plath might think about the flood of ink that has been expended on her story, I will venture that she would want her case to be championed by someone with a better command of English than Paul Alexander displays. He will perform almost any syntactical contortion rather than end a sentence, or even a clause, with a preposition: "From wherever she came, Plath arrived in Cambridge on October 1—alone." Or: "But above all, she needed a good au-pair girl, Sylvia wrote to her mother on the 16th, a candidate for which she would soon interview."

Malice toward Ted Hughes and his family is nothing new in the history of Plath biography. The most notorious document is Robin Morgan's poem "Arraignment," which begins:

How can
I accuse
Ted Hughes
of what the entire British and American
literary and critical establishment
has been at great lengths to deny,
without ever saying it in so many words, of course:
the murder of Sylvia Plath?

and concludes by entertaining the possibility that she and her
friends might

one night ring the doorbell
to enter, a covey of his girlish fans,
who then disarm him of that weapon with which he
tortured us,
stuff it into his mouth, sew up his poetasting lips around it,
and blow out his brains.
Who knows?

I am not suggesting that Paul Alexander's malice is quite as virulent or as stupid as that. He operates more through innuendo
than accusation. The Plath estate bears, in fact, some of the responsibility for his method, since by refusing permission to
quote freely from copyrighted and unpublished materials, they
put authors like Alexander in the position of suggesting things
he is not in a position to verify.

*Rough Magic* is full of suggestions like: "Obviously, Olwyn was
extremely jealous of Sylvia. Writing to her mother, Sylvia speculated why. Ted and Olwyn were abnormally close, she said. One
could even describe their relationship as incestuous, since they
had slept in the same bed until Olwyn was a young teenager."
Does this mean that brother and sister had committed incest, or
is the word "incestuous" being used loosely? If the latter, then
why are we told they slept in the same bed? And who is the "one"
who "could even describe" the Hughes siblings this way? Is
Alexander paraphrasing Sylvia Plath's letter, or is the author
speaking, or is this a more generalized "one"? A look at the
book's notes tells us: "The information in the next three paragraphs comes from Plath's published and unpublished letters to

her mother, from *Bitter Fame,* and from my interviews with Olwyn Hughes." This serves only to frustrate any attempt at verification the reader might undertake.

I find Alexander's handling of the material both factually unsatisfactory and ethically questionable. Another example where paraphrase leads to ambiguity: "One reason Plath wanted a legal separation, she told Aurelia, was to force Ted to pay the children's daily expenses. Finally, Sylvia could not control her fury. She did not want her children to have a liar and an adulterer for a father, she wrote to her mother. But they did." Whose statement is that last sentence?

Alexander is no more convincing as a psychologist than he is as a moralist. By the most roundabout way imaginable, he hints that Hughes is a repressed homosexual. First he sketches a picture of Hughes's circle in Cambridge. Then, he draws on "an unpublished sequence of short stories" by Daniel Weissbort, "including one—'only slightly fictionalized'—that dealt with the interplay of the young men in this group. In the story, the narrator's psychiatrist tries to explain the give-and-take of the young men. The group is, according to the doctor, 'homosexually collusive'—a term that cast, the narrator says, 'a somewhat ambiguous light over what I had regarded as a peculiarly heroic and male collection of individuals.'"

Having dropped this rather ponderous hint, he can describe Hughes's reaction to a Truman Capote reading: "Ted hated, Sylvia observed, 'the homosexual part of [Capote] with more than usual fury.' Though she saw this, she did not speculate what Ted's attitude revealed, nor did she specify what kind of man is threatened by another man's obvious displays of the feminine side of his personality." Thank you, Dr. Ruth.

Having brought up the subject of hypnotism early in his narrative of Plath's marriage to Hughes, Alexander weaves it into his story. "Think how cool this will be in the movie," you can see him thinking. On their honeymoon "Ted succumbed to sunstroke and Sylvia came down with a severe case of dysentery. Hypnotizing her, Ted planted in her mind a subliminal message: she should sleep soundly that night and wake up feeling better the next day . . . The mind control worked. In the morning, Sylvia awoke with no symptoms of her illness whatsoever."

In much the same way, our author plants that phrase "mind control" in our minds. To what purpose? A rather sinister one. The Friday before the Monday Plath killed herself, she and Ted Hughes met briefly. Shortly after that, friends noticed "a decided change in her personality. Her actions were direct and purposeful, as if after much uncertainty some vital issue had been settled." One might surmise she had made the decision to attempt suicide again. Maybe Hughes had told her that Assia Wevill, the woman he had left her for, was pregnant: that would have convinced her that a reconciliation between her and her husband was now impossible. Alexander adds a further speculation that chills me to the bone with its venomous innuendo:

> Or, as friends of Sylvia's later speculated, perhaps something more ominous occurred Friday night at Fitzroy Road. After years of repeatedly being hypnotized by Ted and acting on his posthypnotic suggestions, Sylvia was highly sensitive to any signal—conscious or unconscious—that she perceived him to be sending. Several times during the fall she had told her mother that Ted wanted her to kill herself; if she believed this, it might have propelled her on some new and purposeful path of action tonight.

Thus, in so many words Paul Alexander, like Robin Morgan, accuses Ted Hughes of murdering his wife—though he hedges his suggestion about the hypnotic signal. On what evidence? "The information in the rest of this paragraph is based in part on *Bitter Fame* and on my interviews with two confidential sources," his note reads. This accusation is too serious—even when couched obliquely—to be based on "confidential sources." The skulking tone, the reliance on dark hints, are characteristic of this book.

The premise of *The Haunting of Sylvia Plath,* by Jacqueline Rose, is that "Sylvia Plath haunts our culture," illuminating and even anticipating debates that are currently in vogue, such as the conflicting claims of art and popular culture, the relations between women's sexual fantasies and gender-based power relations—to name only two. It suits the author's convenience to say that "execrated and idolised, Plath hovers between the furthest poles of positive and negative appraisal." Such a dichotomy misrepresents the appraisal of readers of poetry whom I am aware of. The personal vendettas voiced by some of Anne Stevenson's informants in *Bitter Fame* are, it seems to me, exceptions to, and perhaps even represent envious reactions to, the high esteem in which Plath's late poetry is almost universally held.

It is true that "there are those who pathologise Plath, freely diagnose her as schizophrenic or psychotic, read her writings as symptom or warning, something we should both admire and avoid." Does it follow, as Rose goes on to assert, that "the spectre of psychic life rises up in her person as a monumental affront for which she is punished"? I think not. Readers are more likely to feel pity or wonder. A simpler way to formulate the debate: Was she primarily writing about her inner or her outer experiences? Anne Stevenson asserts that "Plath's true subject was this inner self, not her outer experiences and achievements." Rose counters:

> Feminism has rightly responded to this form of criticism by stressing the representative nature of Plath's inner drama, the extent to which it focuses the inequities (the pathology) of a patriarchal world. But in so doing, it has tended to inherit the framework of the critical language it seeks to reject. Plath becomes innocent—man and patriarchy are to blame. More important, psychic life is stripped of its own logic; it becomes the pure effect of social injustice, wholly subservient to the outside world which it unfailingly reflects.

In this book "feminism" is presented as a monolithic, unnuanced body of opinion, when in reality the term must embrace thousands of varying positions.

Like everyone else, Rose finds herself drawn into the Plath enigma: "One of the strangest effects," she writes, of reading *Bitter Fame* "is that it precisely becomes impossible to know whom to believe." This doesn't prevent her from loading the dice when it suits her purpose. In a letter to her patron Olive Prouty, Plath referred to Ted Hughes as "a breaker of things and people." Accuracy is not served by Rose's saying, "she expresses her fear of his destructiveness as she sees it, his reputation—in her terms—as *seducer and blaster of women and things*" (my italics).

Plath was overwhelmingly concerned with the question that haunts all artists when evaluating their own work—"Is this any good?" For Rose, this is a non-question. She just cannot grasp why Plath agreed with her editor at Knopf to omit all but two sections of her "Poem for a Birthday" from *The Colossus*. The poem is embarrassingly derivative of Theodore Roethke (a major influence on both Plath and Hughes), almost to the point of parody or pastiche. Ted Hughes has called the poem "a deliberate Roethke pastiche, something light and throwaway to begin with, but [it] might lead to something else."

> Let me sit in a flowerpot,
> The spiders won't notice.
> My heart is a stopped geranium.
>
> If only the wind would leave my lungs alone.
> Dogbody noses the petals. They bloom upside down.
> They rattle like hydrangea bushes.

Rose comments that "the criticism that Plath is derivative seems to be absolutely pointless in a context where the engendering of language . . . is what is being represented inside the text. In fact the poem could be said to stage the pre-Oedipal version of the anxiety of influence—the question being not what she took from Roethke but what it is about taking and giving, in relation to language, that she uses him to explore." In other words, Rose hasn't the remotest clue as to what goes on when one is writing a poem—nor, apparently, has she any desire to see the poetic process from the poet's point of view.

There are many useful things to be gleaned from this book. Rose shows, for instance, that the editorial omissions made not only by the Hugheses but by Aurelia Plath have given us a less political Sylvia Plath than in fact her journals, letters, and even her Smith College papers show her to have been. Why does *The Bell Jar* begin: "It was a queer, sultry summer, the summer they electrocuted the Rosenbergs, and I didn't know what I was doing in New York"? In part because Plath herself had been a victim of electroshock therapy. But in a well-argued defense of Plath's use of Holocaust imagery in "Daddy," Rose shows that

Jewishness was a consistent preoccupation of Plath's. As a German American during World War II, Plath got a dose of abuse and social ostracism from her schoolmates in that intensely patriotic period when German-bashing was at its height.

Probably the newest and most original insight in *The Haunting of Sylvia Plath* is Rose's discussion of Plath's relation to popular literary culture. Obviously these days, when "cultural studies" seems to be supplanting the study of literature in universities (not only in the U.S.—Rose teaches at London University and the University of Sussex), popular culture is a trendy subject. And this is a very trendy book. Lucas Myers has written that Plath was equally at home chatting about *Mademoiselle* magazine or discussing the poems of Wallace Stevens. Plath's involvement with magazines like the *Saturday Evening Post,* her attempts to write popular novels (she referred to *The Bell Jar* as a "potboiler"), and the lack of attention paid to this aspect of her work, make this a feminist issue, according to Rose, "for feminists have been among the first to point out that the denigration of popular culture carries with it a specific denigration of women." It does help to see Plath within the context of the totality of her writing. Rose seems, however, somewhat to miss the point of Plath's own priorities: "I can write for the women's slicks: More and more this comes over me—as easily as I wrote for *Seventeen,* while keeping my art intact." Not surprisingly in the current climate of literary theory (Rose is a fierce one for attacking "high-art pretension"), art gets little respect in these pages.

The book's effort is to unstick the debate surrounding Sylvia Plath from the pathology/patriarchy question, which she sums up as follows: "Pathology . . . makes her guilty—her tragedy the inevitable outcome of the troubles of her mind. Patriarchy means that man, meaning Hughes or the male sex he stands for, is to blame—the woman internalises, turns against herself, the violence of the world outside." Still, I was a bit startled to read, "In this book, in the analysis of those writings, I am never talking of real people, but of textual entities (Y and X) whose more than real reality, I will be arguing, goes beyond them to encircle us all. It has been objected that writing on Plath is a fantasia with no purchase on, or even interest in, the truth. This book starts from the assumption that Plath is a fantasy." Perhaps there are readers who feel comfortable with this assumption. Plath, Hughes, and most of the important minor characters in their tragedy are dead now. I can't forget—*don't want to forget*—that they once lived and breathed, not as fantasies but as human beings.

# Blueberries Sprinkled with Salt
## *Frost's Letters*

"Why go on and write poems, obscure what has already been done. Too many writers bury themselves in the rubbish of their old age. Any prolific writer runs the risk of becoming 'common' and 'popular' . . . Critics like to think of a 'poet's poet.' I can see some of them are already wavering . . . I'm getting too popular for them." Frost said this to his friend and former student John Bartlett in 1932. He was fifty-eight, the author of five volumes of poetry, the recipient of two Pulitzer prizes. In his old age Frost's serious audience wavered more and more. This estrangement, even as Frost described it to Bartlett, was manifold: partly attributable to the "rubbish" he sometimes wrote (the Masques, for example), partly a modish reaction to his popularity, but mainly a result of the figure he cut playing, as Elizabeth Isaacs admiringly puts it, "poet-sage of the century." When the poet-sage charmed his *Saturday Evening Post* audience with his comparisons between poetry and baseball, one felt like Frost's mad sister Jeanie: "She took me for someone else when she saw me. She shouted to me by name to save her from whoever she thought I was in person." The poet-sage damaged the critical reputation of his poems so much that Randall Jarrell's two fine essays in his *Poetry and the Age* (1953) were sorely needed propaganda for Frost as a serious poet.

Lawrance Thompson, the editor of this collection, notes that in the letters Frost "carries himself primarily as lyric poet," expressing temporary stances rather than fixed beliefs. He shows

---

Review of *Selected Letters of Robert Frost,* ed. Lawrance Thompson (New York: Henry Holt, 1964). From the *Sewanee Review.*

that, more than the ordinary person, Frost shaped his letters with such subtlety and indirection that one must read particular statements only within the context of the letter (and of course within the larger context of his life and work). Thompson's brief descriptions of the characters involved and Frost's relations with them help to give a balanced view; for unlike the lyric poem the letter is addressed to a specific person.

Of particular interest is the revelation that "The Road Not Taken" was originally written as a letter in verse to Edward Thomas, the English poet with whom Frost became friends while living in England. The poem was intended to satirize Thomas's style and attitudes. The line "I shall be telling this with a sigh" was to be a dead giveaway, since Frost thought "wasted regret" sentimental and unmanly. Perhaps the poem ran away with him, however, for Thomas missed the joke, as did the American audiences to whom Frost repeatedly hinted, "You have to be careful of that one; it's a tricky poem—very tricky." Like the knowledge that the last stanza of Matthew Arnold's "Dover Beach" was written years before the rest of the poem, this information may cause a complicated critical problem, unless you invoke the "intentional fallacy" and simply ignore it. In discouraging Sidney Cox from writing a second book about him, Frost wrote: "I have written to keep the over curious out of the secret places of my mind both in my verse and in my letters to such as you. A subject has to be held clear outside of me with struts and as it were set up for an object. A subject must be an object . . . My objection to your larger book about me was that it came thrusting in where I did not want you."

A myth of biography has surrounded the figure of Frost from early on. One attractive feature of the "Frost story" has been his period of preparation as poet. The following account from one biographer may be taken as typical: "When he was nineteen, Robert Frost made known to his grandfather a wish to become a poet. Grandfather William Prescott Frost offered to let him try his poetry for a year. If the poetry was not a success, there were other things for a worthy young grandson to do. Robert's reply to the offer of a year was prophetic: 'Give me twenty,' he said." Add to this a quotation from "The Road Not Taken" and the appeal is familiar. According to this account, Frost is seen as content to take the road less traveled by, write his poetry as he pleased, and let recognition come whenever it felt like it.

The truth, as usual, is less simple. The twelve years Frost spent farming near Derry and teaching at Pinkerton were crucial in the formation of his character, though he was not to achieve poetical maturity until he moved to England. He supplemented his inherited annuity by farming and journalism before settling down to teaching. In a supposedly factual piece of reporting for a poultry magazine he rather violated the actual by claiming that his neighbor's geese "roost in the trees even in winter." Another Yankee farmer wrote the magazine: "Now I am 45 years old and have been among geese all my life time, and I can never remember seeing a goose in a tree. I thought if I could get a breed of that kind I could dispense with coops." Frost tried to squelch the controversy by going above it, so to speak: "Geese would sleep out, or float out, let us say, where hens would roost in the trees. To be sure. But what more natural, in speaking of geese in close connection with hens, than to speak of them as if they were hens? 'Roost in the trees,' has here simply suffered what the grammarians would call attraction from the subject with which it should be in agreement to the one uppermost in mind. That is all."

He followed this up with a letter signed by his semi-literate neighbor to dissipate the issue with other tactics: "I once had a duck that laid her eggs in a tree high enough to be out of reach from the ground, and brought off twenty-two ducklings. These were Brazilians, and I don't know what they won't do. It has always seemed strange to me how people succeed in keeping geese shut up. If I shut mine up they begin to be restless right away, and go off in looks, especially plumage. Mr. White needn't think because I let my geese run wild I think any less of them than other folks. They are good ones . . ." I quote this at length not deliberately to introduce the trivial, but to give an indication of one sort of thing Frost was doing in these years, and also to show how essentially non-Yankee the New England bard could be. Six children were born to the Frosts in this period and two of them died. The family suffered from sickness, loneliness, and poverty; and Frost had published only ten poems over a period of eighteen years. In addition he was worn-out with teaching just as he had become fed-up with farming. As he wrote

Bartlett after leaving New Hampshire, "Gone out of the rabbit business, hey? Ain't working the land? Easier to write about it? Think I don't understand?"

They sold their farm and went to England. Within two months Frost had found a publisher for *A Boy's Will:* "I brought it to England in the bottom of my trunk . . . I came here to write rather than to publish." Be that as it may, he immediately began to promote the book in London literary circles. Part of a letter to Bartlett gives the tone of his excitement:

> I am in mortal fear now lest the reviewers should fail to take any notice of it . . . It has brought me several exciting friendships which I can tell you about without exciting any jealousy in your breast because you know that I care more for you and your opinion of me (formed when I was fifteenth in command at Pinkerton) than for the opinion of all the rest of them put together. Yeats has asked me to make one of his circle at his Monday Nights when he is in London (and not in Dublin). And he told my dazzling friend Ezra Pound that my book was the best thing that has come out of America for some time. Of course we needn't believe that. I spent the evening with Yeats in his dark-curtained candlelit room last week . . . And Ezra Pound, the stormy petrel, I must tell you more about him when I have more time. He has found me and sent a fierce article to Chicago denouncing a country that neglects fellows like me. I am afraid he over did it and it may be a mercy all round if it isn't printed. It is likely to be though as he always seems to have his way with the magazine it has gone to [*Poetry*]. All this ought to be enough to satisfy me for the time being you will think. But dear dear. The boom is not started yet.

Frost followed up his London success by sending copies of favorable reviews to friends in America and coaxing them to get him reviewed on this side of the Atlantic. He developed a talent for making suggestions to a would-be reviewer in a form that the reviewer could easily copy. John Bartlett received these friendly instructions:

> Well then in August, say, as soon as you get *The Bookman* you can begin a little article for Morse-back of *The News and Enterprise* like this:

Former pupils of R. F. at Pink may be interested to learn of the success of his first book published in London. A recent number of *The Bookman* (Eng.) contains etc.—You are not to get the least bit enthusiastic—I know you my child. Keep strictly to the manner of the disinterested reporter. Make the article out of the reviews almost entirely. In mentioning *The English Review* you might mention the fact that it is a leading literary monthly here.

Even though it took a bit of pushing on Frost's part to get the right things said about his first books, they deserved the praise they got. He was an abnormally proud and sensitive man, he had waited a long time for his turn, and he naturally wanted to make the most of it when it came. All his life Frost was jealous of public esteem, and the distinction between a "somebody" and a "nobody" was important to him. On a visit to Vermont in 1928, Bartlett was taking Frost for a drive and had "started the wrong way up a one-way street. He'd shifted into reverse when a shiny Buick with New York license plates pulled alongside, with a nattily dressed driver at the wheel. 'What do you think you're doing?' he asked, flashing his gold teeth. 'Who are you?' answered Frost, glaring. 'You're going the wrong way,' the stranger answered, still baring his gold teeth. 'Who are you? Please introduce yourself before you speak to us!'"

Recent criticism has concerned itself with discovering the "dark side" of Frost's poetry. This is valuable, but in a sense the emphasis is misplaced, because in much of his poetry the pessimism is not stated, but merely suggested. Basically a pessimistic person, Frost probably needed his poetical pep-talks more than his audience needed them. His life was surrounded by personal tragedy. His family was plagued by illness, including tuberculosis and insanity. I have mentioned his unfortunate sister Jeanie; Frost must have seen his own tendencies carried over the brink in the acuteness and schizophrenic brilliance of her letters written from the insane asylum where she finally died: "I am very peculiar and did not start right . . . People always slight me . . . I've hardly ever been pleased at anything else in my life except when I drank coffee or when people praised me . . . The universe seems only a machine to me, flowers, books, and everything, or

*97*

else long drawn out obsequies. The first is the worst . . . Everything almost I read or look at seems to me like eating blueberries slightly sprinkled with salt."

He worried that his dedication to his art was causing him either to neglect or to dominate the members of his family: "Do I exercise a soft tyranny? I've never had any trouble with any one of them. They speak out so seldom that it astonishes me when one does." A particular source of grief was his son, Carol. Frost seems never to have understood him. He mentioned to the Bartletts the notion of buying Carol a sheep farm in Colorado: "Maybe I'm foolish to be thinking of it. Carol seemed to like the idea, but I don't know how much is for himself, and how much is because I'm urging him to it." When Carol committed suicide in 1940, Frost wrote to Louis Untermeyer:

> I took the wrong way with him. I tried many ways and every single one of them was wrong. Some thing in me is still asking for the chance to try one more . . . Two weeks ago I was up at South Shaftsbury telling Carol how to live. Yesterday I was telling seven hundred Harvard freshmen how to live with books in college. Apparently nothing can stop us once we get going. I talk less and less however as if I knew what I was talking about . . . I failed to trick Carol or argue him into believing he was the least successful. That's what it came down to. He failed in farming and he failed in poetry (you may not have known). He was splendid with animals and little children. If only the emphasis could have been put on those. He should have lived with horses.

The beautiful person in these letters is Frost's wife, Elinor. Shortly before her death he wrote: "She has been the unspoken half of everything I ever wrote, and both halves of many a thing from My November Guest down to the last stanzas of Two Tramps in Mud Time—as you may have divined." To get her tone would take more quoting than there is room for here— but an impression of what she must have been like grows from reading Frost's love poems. In a letter to Untermeyer correcting mistakes he thought Amy Lowell had made about him in an article written when he was first becoming known in America, he remarked:

That's an unpardonable attempt to do her as the conventional helpmate of genius. Elinor has never been of any earthly use to me. She hasn't cared whether I went to school or worked or earned anything . . . She wouldn't lift a hand or have me lift a hand to increase my reputation or even save it. And this isn't all from devotion to my art at its highest. She seems to have the same weakness I have for a life that goes rather poetically; only I should say she is worse than I. It isn't what might be expected to come from such a life—poetry that she is after. And it isn't that she doesn't think I am a good poet either. She always knew I was a good poet, but that was between her and me . . . Catch her getting any satisfaction out of what her housekeeping may have done to feed a poet! Rats!

Here are the Frosts at a literary conference in 1932: "The freedom of his conversation was watched over by Elinor, who would say, 'Don't Robert!' if she thought his comment improper. (He didn't.)" She was not so strong as her husband, nor so flexible. Frost, for one thing, was almost apolitical, though tending toward a liberal populism, like his father; she opposed the New Deal vigorously—this, her heart trouble, the family sorrows, all gave her a sense of things closing in. The same account continues: "I remember sitting on the bench under our apple tree talking to Elinor. Her voice was quiet, her eyes tearful, but without tears. In her hands she clutched a ball of a handkerchief and an abused pack of cigarettes. She seemed cool, distant, and her smile was only a remote suggestion, as if she meant 'some other time, not now.'" After her death from angina in 1938 her husband wrote:

It is now running into more than a week longer than I was ever away from her since June 1895 . . .

I suppose love must always deceive. I'm afraid I deceived her a little in pretending for the sake of argument that I didn't think the world as bad a place as she did. My excuse was that I wanted to keep her a little happy for my own selfish pleasure. It is as if for the sake of argument she had sacrificed her life to give me this terrible answer and really bring me down in sorrow. She needn't have. I knew I never had a leg to stand on, and I should think I had said so in print.

Frost's own working theory of poetry, developed over the years, is perhaps the most valuable single thing in his letters. Writing to Bartlett from England in 1913 he said: "To be perfectly frank with you I am one of the most notable craftsmen of my time. That will transpire presently. I am possibly the only person going who works on any but a worn out theory (principle I had better say) of versification." Good poetry must contain the "sound of sense," the essence of a sound heard in conversation that convinces you unconsciously that something familiar and meaningful is being said. Frost thought this essence could be heard by listening to a conversation behind a closed door, where the exact words could not be distinguished.

But this "sound of sense" was only the raw material for poetry; the trick was to "get cadences by skillfully breaking the sounds of sense with all their irregularity of accent across the regular beat of the metre." Verse with only the metrical beat would be doggerel; with only the speech accent it would be only speech. The theory was extended: "I give you a new definition of a sentence: A sentence is a sound in itself on which other sounds called words may be strung . . . A man is all writer if all his words are strung on definite recognizable sentence sounds. The voice of the imagination, the speaking voice must know certainly how to behave, how to posture in every sentence he offers."

This set of principles, given here in a sketchy form, will take its place alongside a handful of other highly individual theories of poetry passed on to us by such working masters as Ben Jonson, Pope, Keats, Wordsworth, Hopkins, and Eliot. Let me entertain a few quibbles and speculations, however. Must the strictly formal iambic (or other) meter be a necessary component of verse? Wouldn't the sound of sense ring just as true in unmetered verse? Remove the iambics, and the theory applies also to such free verse artists as W. C. Williams, Marianne Moore, Robert Creeley, and W. S. Merwin. Also, it seems arbitrary to introduce the criterion of the sentence; can't the "voice of the imagination" make itself heard as much in a single word or phrase (in context) as in a sentence?

With certain modifications Frost's ideas seem to open up greater innovations than he himself effected, though of course he was not interested in this kind of innovation. "One of my prides," he wrote, "is that I can write a fifty word telegram without having to use a single 'Stop' for the sense." If this is true, and if the speaking voice must know how to read each line, then wouldn't a logical extension be to do away with punctuation altogether? Frost would not like to know that his idiosyncratically acute theory was being used to encourage experiment, but it is conceivable some of the younger poets might have him as a reluctant guide.

# In Praise of Rhyme

What draws us to poetry in our early, inarticulate years? Answers to the question must vary. From the days when, as a child, I passively absorbed poetry from songs and hymns and when, as an adolescent, I tried to write things of my own in imitation of poems from books, I recall the delicious pleasure that rhymes gave: a sense of suspended attention, like a child's brainy and indolent imaginings. Partial or slant rhymes pleased me more than full rhymes: when "door," shall we say, chimed with "ajar," the echo effect rang deeper than when the rhymes were full and obvious. Here is a verse from a hymn:

> We blossom and flourish
> Like leaves on the tree,
> Then wither and perish,
> But naught changes Thee.

Surely this hymnbook versifier, whatever his name may be, knew what he was about, weaving together the graceful, complex feminine rhymes "flourish" and "perish," letting them stand for the impermanence of mortal life when sounded against the simple, open-voweled monoliths of "tree" and "Thee."

The hymnal, though, with its complacencies and reassurances, is not the best place to look for partial rhymes, which seem to have come into being in the service of modern poets who, if they wanted in their verses the musicality of rhyme, needed a wider range of choice than is afforded by the stringencies of full rhyme. (Obviously English lacks the easy rhymes of the Romance languages, with their generic endings: cha-

---

From *Ploughshares*.

peau/chateau, etc.) As far as I can see, though there are earlier examples—the English and Scottish ballads, notably—Emily Dickinson gave the gift of partial rhyme to modern poets (remember that her poetry became widely known only in the 1920s). The slant rhymes of Wilfred Owen's World War I poetry had reached readers only a few years before Dickinson's work, freed of the emendations that regularized her unruly rhymes, became widely known. In quatrains like the following, Dickinson uses her subtle half-rhymes (spelled/dead) to place a casual churchyard stroll within death's solemn domain:

> Weeds triumphant ranged
> Strangers strolled and spelled
> At the lone Orthography
> Of the Elder Dead

But I wonder if any poet has ever had an ear equal to that of John Crowe Ransom. Spectacularly unfashionable now, damningly associated in readers' minds with the New Criticism of the 1940s and 1950s, Ransom was Robert Lowell's mentor at Kenyon College and must have contributed mightily to the education of Lowell's own superb musical sense. Here is the opening of "Bells for John Whiteside's Daughter":

> There was such speed in her little body,
> And such lightness in her footfall,
> It is no wonder her brown study
> Astonishes us all.

"Body" and "study" are the most delicate of feminine rhymes. Ransom, as it were, levitates the lovely word "footfall," preparing the reader's ear with the delicately trochaic ( / *) "lightness," which is where the pitch of the line peaks. Our "mind's ear" can't quite decide whether to accent "footfall" on the first syllable or on both syllables, and that hesitation produces a kind of hovering accent. In the first line as well, the pitch peaks at the word "speed"; thus in both lines the end-rhyme tries musically to maintain itself at the level of pleasurable intensity achieved in the middle of both lines, like a youngest son trying to jump as high as his brothers.

The singsong monotony of iambics written by someone with an inadequate musical sense is the death of the metrical line, and no one was more emphatic in his avoidance of this monotony than Ransom, who spoke of "roughing up" the iambics. The lines we are looking at could be scanned several different ways. It's hard to say whether the first line is iambic pentameter or whether it's a three-beat accentual line. Similarly, is the second line tetrameter, or is it also a three-beat accentual? The way the lines lightly sway between strict and loose rhythms, like the silken tent in Robert Frost's poem of the same name, "astonishes us" just as surely as does the little girl's death, spoken of in a phrase typical of Ransom's characteristically archaic rhetoric as "her brown study," which my dictionary calls "a state of deep thought, melancholy, or reverie." It's an expression my grandmother in Tennessee used.

The traditional language of prosody, which I have dipped into here with just the tip of my nib, has a rough usefulness, but can only point, like a finger pointed toward the moon, at the verbal music that we hear in the lines of poets like Dickinson, Ransom, Herrick, and Keats. Should we for the sake of precision adopt the more elaborate, computer-assisted prosodic approaches offered by modern linguistics? For some people these approaches are productive. For me the mad-scientist language of linguistics is just too complicated, and, besides, it takes the enjoyably amateur, slightly bumbling fun out of scanning poetry. In praising rhyme my aim is to praise an amateur enthusiasm—i.e., the enthusiasm of a lover—about the details and traditions of poetry, on the part of poets who write freely as well as poets who write formally. Rhyme, when it works, is a matter of pleasure.

Try to talk about a few pairs of rhymes and you find yourself discussing rhythm. Etymologists say that the more correct spelling "rime" was subverted somewhere along the line by association with the word "rhythm," both derived from the Latin word "rhythmus," which like most words having to do with art, was plundered directly from Greek.

Where did rhyme come from? Classical poets, Homer and Virgil for instance, did not use it. We know that our own Anglo-Saxon predecessors did not rhyme their poems, but instead used a very serviceable pattern of alliteration. In his famous versification class at Harvard, Robert Fitzgerald used to talk about the marching songs sung by the Roman legions on the road home from Gaul as rhyme's first incursion into the Classical tradition, the supposition being that the rhyming in these songs was influenced by the folk poetry of the Gauls. Rhyme also appears in the Medieval Latin poems of the *Carmina Burana*.

It would seem, then, that in European literature, rhyme is a property of modern, as distinguished from classical, poetry. Yet Irish poets, as far back at least as the fifth century and probably beyond that, made up rhymes; so we can assume that it was a feature of the Celtic culture which was dominant in Europe in the first millennium B.C. Rhyme's occurrence in diverse Indo-European literatures suggests that its absence in Greek and Latin poetry constitutes the exception rather than the rule in cultures stretching from Ireland in the West to India in the East.

On the psychic level, rhyme's appeal must have something to do with our instinctual taste for periodicity and return, the regular rising and setting of the sun, the sound of two hands clapping, a pair of aces. Just now, on the top branch of the pear tree that grows over the stone wall at the foot of our garden here in Ireland, a male bullfinch alighted. As I was admiring his stout bill, his watered-pink waistcoat, his burgher's prosperous midsection, the female flew briskly over the wall and joined him, jostling the fellow slightly as she perched—the pair of them like a banker and his wife settling down in their box at the theater. That's rhyme.

# Louis Simpson
*The Poet of the 5:51*

"It has come true," reads the first Louis Simpson poem that I encountered some twenty years ago,

> The journey and the danger of the
>> world,
>> All that there is
> To bear and to enjoy, endure and do.
> ("My Father in the Night Commanding No")

A fitting summary of Simpson's poetry. Reading his recent work one wants to add—sticking to the rhyme scheme—"and suburbia too."

Having been from the beginning an admirably "impure" poet (to borrow Czeslaw Milosz's sly term for Whitman, Shakespeare, Homer, Dante, et al., as opposed to those modern poets who aspire to an art of "pure" imagination), Simpson has taken on the challenge of trying to make sense of contemporary life, from his soldiering experiences in World War II to American historical myths and realities—wherein "The Open Road goes to the used-car lot." Increasingly, he writes about ordinary characters and their everyday experiences. Simpson stoutly refuses the pressure from "purists" to force poetry into a limited and marginal role. The title of his selected poems, *People Live Here,* is an indication of this writer's determination to engage his imagination with characterization and plot.

For him, as for Matthew Arnold, poetry has been a "criticism

---

Review of *People Live Here* (New York: Boa Editions, 1983) and *The Best Hour of the Night* (Boston: Houghton Mifflin, 1983). From the *Nation.*

of life." Simpson has consistently chosen a large canvas; his poetry is various, compassionate, committed, and often astonish-
ingly beautiful. He is adept enough—and I would say, humane
enough (I take the will to communicate as a gauge of an artist's
humanity)—to be clear and readable. If the rhetorical intensity
of his poems slackens in the process, it should also be noted that
their plainness of diction contributes to their directness.

One is struck over and over both by the range of subject and
treatment and by the unifying effect of Louis Simpson's voice
and attitude on heterogeneous material. While capable of lyric
rapture, this poet typically holds himself at some distance from
his subjects and is by turns satirical, bemused, sorrowing, dis-
dainful, sympathetic, wry. Yet to say that he holds himself at some
distance is less accurate than to note that while sympathetic,
Simpson seems by his very nature to be an outsider. He grew up
in Jamaica, West Indies, with parents of Scottish and Russian de-
scent; he was seventeen before he moved to the United States.
While he engages himself passionately with American life, at
times it is as if the poet were an anthropologist from an alien culture observing American ways. Simpson was the alien Easterner
in California, for instance, two decades before Annie Hall:

> Here I am, troubling the dream coast
> With my New York face,
> Bearing among the realtors
> And tennis-players my dark pre-occupation.
>
> ("In California")

And here is his account of certain Long Island folkways:

> There aren't too many alternatives.
> The couple sitting in the car
> will either decide to go home
> or to a motel.
> Afterwards, they may continue
> to see each other, in which case
> there will probably be a divorce,
> or else they may decide
> to stop seeing each other.
>
> ("Little Colored Flags")

His attitude is deadpan, insistently noncommittal. In "American Classic" he addresses the issue of alienation:

> The feeling of being left out
> through no fault of your own, is common.
> That's why I say, an American classic.

*The Best Hour of the Night* reflects Simpson's increasing focus on life in the suburbs. "Suburbia" is a word rarely mentioned without an implied sneer, but to dismiss or ignore it is to eliminate from consideration a significant slice of the American pie. As Robert Lowell put it, "History has to live with what was here." Someone who knew nothing of present-day America would get little idea of our life from most contemporary poetry. I often think of a student of mine some years ago who said, "I never feel completely at ease outside of Great Neck," and I can almost imagine her in a Simpson poem. His view of these briefcase-carriers, deal-strikers, Saturday-night poker players and village-meeting-goers combines detachment with a self-effacing sense of identification.

In his examination of *Homo suburbanus,* Simpson does not avoid the iffy area of morality. "Do you know the eleventh commandment?" Harry, one of his characters, asks. (The eleventh commandment is "Don't get caught.") After Harry makes this remark, the poet, almost but not quite a straight man, notes coolly: "Then, as I recall, everyone laughs." Harry is later sent to prison for

> kickbacks, misapplication of funds,
> conspiracy, fraud, concealment, wire fraud,
> falsified books and records, and
> interstate transportation of stolen property.
> ("The Eleventh Commandment")

The poem concludes with the poet's dry comment on greeting Harry's young son after the father's removal: "'Hi there,' I say to him. / What else do you say to a six-year-old?"

In staking out fresh material for his poetry, it is not surprising that Louis Simpson should feel the necessity of creating new or at least hybrid forms. This he has done notably in "The Previous Tenant," which is something like a short story in free verse. The form allows the writer to highlight certain details without being bound to the three-dimensional realism and continuity of traditional fiction. The speaker rents a cottage where the previous tenant has left some of his belongings, and through conversations with the landlord and others, he pieces together the story of an affair his predecessor had that caused all sorts of trouble including the divorce that necessitated his moving into the cottage in the first place. It's a fascinating, skillfully spun tale in which we learn all sorts of different things about the characters involved, the speaker, the little suburban town in which the story is set, and, finally, about American values. As Simpson says in "Walt Whitman at Bear Mountain":

> all the realtors,
> Pickpockets, salesmen, and the actors performing
> Official scenarios,
> Turned a deaf ear, for they had contracted
> American dreams.

# Philip Levine
## *Working the Night Shift*

Among the poems in *One for the Rose,* the lightning-strike of poetic authenticity is unmistakable in "Belief." This poem asserts
by denying—using the recurring motif, "No one believes," to
capture the ambivalent attitude we take toward things we somehow believe while "knowing" they cannot be true. While insisting upon denial, the poem creates a detailed, compelling vision:

> No one believes that to die
> is beautiful, that after the hard pain
> of the last unsaid word I am swept
> in a calm out from shore
> and hang in the silence of millions
> for the first time among all my family.

If no other single poem in the book quite matches the achievement of "Belief," there is much to like in *One for the Rose.* Philip
Levine's poems have the rare and laudable virtue of readability;
they carry the charm and vitality of the poet's distinctive speaking
voice, which is by turns assertive and tough or humorously self-
deprecatory.

Mr. Levine has been called a blue-collar poet, and it is true
that he typically presents himself as a young man from the poor
streets of Detroit, working the night shift at some place like "Detroit Transmission." But even among scenes like "the oily floors /
of filling stations where our cars / surrendered their lives and we
called / it quits and went on foot," the speaker is never a blue-

---

Review of *One for the Rose* (Pittsburgh: Carnegie Mellon University Press,
1999). From the *New York Times Book Review.*

collar caricature, but someone with brains, feelings, and a free-wheeling imagination that constantly fights to free him from his prosaic environment, as in these first lines from "I Was Born in Lucerne":

> Everyone says otherwise. They take me
> to a flat on Pingree in Detroit
> and say, up there, the second floor. I say,
> No, in a small Italian hotel overlooking
> the lake.

Levine's poems are notable for his quick eye and deft turn of phrase, as when he notices "the dew that won't wait long enough / to stand my little gray wren a drink."

The other side of this poet's accessibility is a frequent flatness of diction and an over-reliance on the line break for emphasis, but those are practically generic faults in contemporary American poetry. The repetitive rhetorical device that is so effective in "Belief" is unconvincing in some other poems. Another weakness is his reliance on easy rhetorical clinchers such as "Somewhere I am a God. / Somewhere I am a holy / object. Somewhere I am." But even his least successful efforts have their appeal. No reader of poetry would want to do without these gritty, funny, deeply engaged poems that take on the world as it comes. As Philip Levine describes the events of his life, "each one smells like an overblown rose, / yellow, American, beautiful, and true."

# Household Economy, Ruthlessness, Romance, and the Art of Hospitality
*Notes on Revision*

> Intensely hot. I made pies in the morning. William
> went into the wood and altered his poems.
> —Dorothy Wordsworth,
> journal entry for July 28, 1800

To revise is to improve, and I suspect that the desire to improve hints at a longing for perfection, which shows how related the formal and spiritual sides of poetry can be. The impulse to improve is also a sign of humility, of bowing one's neck before the humbling undertaking of learning how to be worth one's salt as a writer. Humility is naturally rare, particularly among young writers, for whom the value of doing something remarkable is vastly increased if they can claim it took very little time to accomplish.

A friend once gave me photocopies of Elizabeth Bishop's worksheets for her villanelle "One Art," and I have looked at Robert Lowell's early drafts of "Skunk Hour" in Houghton Library at Harvard. In their inception these masterpieces showed, on paper at least (and where else is one to look?), few sparks of genius, few notes of originality or distinctive voice. "Skunk Hour" being notable for its gradual and seemingly inevitable progression of stanzas, it's surprising to see that the last few stanzas came to Lowell first and that the introductory part of the poem was tacked on later. "One Art" being among a handful of perfect villanelles in the language, it's surprising that the poem began as a series of dispirited and formless reflections on what

From *The Practice of Poetry: Writing Exercises from Poets Who Teach*, by Robin Behn and Chase Twichell (New York: HarperResource, 1992).

Bishop would end up calling "the art of losing." These poets were masters of household economy who, upon looking in the fridge and seeing a couple of old potatoes, half a cabbage, and some neglected cheese, could bring to the table a tasty meal based on these scraps. The lesson here is to trust your instincts, to have hope and faith enough to recognize material that you and only you can turn into something savory.

Faith and hope, yes. Charity, no. At least not toward your own material. When you see little spots on the cabbage, throw it out. Ruthlessness, like charity, begins at home. This is hard to learn. Robert Lowell was a great writing teacher because he wasn't shy about telling people hard truths about their own poems. Of a seventeen-line effort: "I think this is a marvelous poem. Cut the first sixteen lines and go from there." The author of the seventeen-liner was unlikely to take offense, knowing that Lowell was even more severe toward his own work.

Get a sense of the poem as something not defined by or limited to the words you have written down in your first few attempts. A good poem, even in potential form, has a shape, a life, that floats above the words: "the light around the body," as Robert Bly put it. Memorizing poems and saying them aloud is a good way to become aware of the poem as a metaverbal entity. Apprehend the poem's field of energy, then think, while revising, of coming at that field from a different direction than you have tried so far. Your poem is a city; instead of getting off the freeway and driving into town straight down Main Street, imagine you're out at the junkyard next to the lake, trying to get hubcaps for your '78 Ford Country Squire. Leave your car there underneath the big maples and walk into town through the railroad freight yards, past the greenhouses, up past the soccer field. In other words, start at line seventeen. Savvy rewriting is a way of staying flexible when entertaining that separate being which is the poem. The metaphor of "entertaining" is deliberate. Being a good host means coming up with fresh things to do that will allow your guest to enjoy herself. And if she's having a good time, well, you take it from there.

If you and your poem like the way it feels when the two of you are sitting together, you will find yourself caught up in the same spirit of inspiration that inclined you to keep company in the first place. Getting back into that spirit, participating in a revision, will keep you from knocking the bloom off your original excitement and making the poem seem worked over. While keeping your options open and allowing the poem to suggest new moves, you'll want to live with your guest twenty-four hours a day. When you wake up in the morning you'll be thinking about the poem; when you come back from the pub at night you'll sit down, read it through, and make a few changes. Revising is not so much a task as it is a romance. I like to write the whole poem out fresh whenever I make changes. That puts me into the flow of the poem, the music of the poem. It's at this point that those assonances, consonances, alliterations, repetitions, that give the poem its subtle music become refined.

Here you rely on the ear you have already developed, and you further educate your ear for work you will do in the future. Sitting down and fine-tuning the poem once it has settled into something like its final form comes at the very end of the process. Like the chocolates, brandy, and cigars that come at the end of the dinner, this phase is the least demanding, most luxurious part. Now you can sit back and enjoy yourself.

# Quincy House and the White House

On a given Wednesday morning sometime in the mid-1960s, six or eight or a dozen poets—most of them young—could be found sitting around a seminar table in a windowless basement room in Quincy House at Harvard. What brought us here was what Robert Lowell called "office hours." Not what their name would suggest, they were a loosely organized conversation to which Lowell's writing students were invited—and also known by word of mouth to other poets in Cambridge and Boston. Lowell would often invite someone he had met at a party. Private chat of a mostly literary nature proceeded quietly within these cinder-block walls, though not so quietly as to preclude eavesdropping. Much of what was said seemed meant to be overheard. A burly man with a patriarchal beard and somewhat menacing manner has just had a poem accepted by the *Nation*. A Radcliffe senior with a chestnut pageboy has just won a grant that will take her to Spain next year.

The man we were waiting for brought to the role of poet in the early 1960s an air of glamour, controversy, and authority not seen since in American literary life. Everyone was reading his 1959 book, *Life Studies,* with its exhilarating writing and painful revelations about its author's psychological difficulties and tumultuous personal life. I had read it in the back seat of my family's Buick on the drive from Memphis to Cambridge to begin graduate school. The Confessional movement was like June, in the sense that it was bursting out all over. Literary magazines that only last week were filled with poems about baroque palazzi and the sun setting over West Egg, now seemed to go in for nervous breakdowns, broken windows, and gin.

From the *Kenyon Review.*

Lowell liked Claude Lévi-Strauss's division of the poetry of the day into the "cooked" and the "raw." You can hear something of the hilarity and unconventional leaps of his conversation in this sentence from his National Book Award acceptance: "The cooked, marvelously expert and remote, seems constructed as a sort of mechanical or catnip mouse for graduate seminars; the raw, jerry-built and forensically deadly, seems often like an un-scored libretto by some bearded but vegetarian Castro." The poem as catnip mouse and the "bearded but vegetarian Castro" are prime examples of the rhetorical hyperbole Lowell enjoyed in conversation. His own writing was more visceral than the cooked, more articulate than the raw.

Two days a week Lowell commuted from Manhattan to Harvard to teach. To our self-regarding New England parish with its good furniture and not entirely unpleasant odor of dry-rot, he brought the electrical charge of a lightning storm. Often the clubby familiarity of our group was disturbed or enlivened by the unfamiliar presence of a visitor: a journalist with an Ox-bridge accent and an Old Something-or-Other tie; or a drop-dead babe wearing a mink coat and a designer ensemble that made our second-hand tweed jackets from Max Keezer's in Central Square look even shabbier than they were.

Robert Lowell, grey-haired, often looking anxious or hung-over, came into the room, slouched into his usual chair, greeted us distractedly with the air of a man who had slept badly, and lit the first of many True cigarettes. He sort of forgot about tending to the cigarette, and his tie and shirt front soon wore a spotty snowfall of ash. Conversation was his meat and drink. As he talked he deployed his hands in a style all his own, molding sentences, pushing outward with his palms, kneading ideas into place as though they were taking shape in the air just inches from his face. He has been described often, but it gives me pleasure to picture my old teacher from many years ago. Despite all his delicacy of gesture, he had the broad shoulders and back of the varsity tackle he had played on the football team at Kenyon College. When his enthusiasm boiled over into one of his manic episodes, it was said that more than a couple or even a few strong men were needed to subdue him.

At office hours we rarely saw Lowell in his manic mode. Our

interaction was routine, good-natured, and businesslike. Some-one would take out a poem, read it aloud, and then pass it up to Lowell at the head of the table. He would then carefully read the poem again in his dry, world-weary voice. His accent has often been remarked upon. As a young man, Lowell left Harvard after his freshman year to apprentice himself to the Southern poet John Crowe Ransom, who was teaching and editing the *Kenyon Review*. From Ransom and Allen Tate, whom he visited in Monteagle, he absorbed certain features of the Southern accent, such as the broad Tennessee "i"—soft, pronounced lower in the throat than the nasal, sharpened, Northern and Midwestern version of that vowel. The accent, part of the young poet's jettisoning of New England in favor of things Southern, must have irritated his Bostonian parents no end. As a graduate student coming to Harvard from Tennessee in 1962, I found his accent reassuringly familiar in that often forbidding East Coast academic world.

Just hearing your poem read aloud in Lowell's voice often told you what was wrong with it. You could hear his intelligence probing the poem's inner architecture, or lack of inner architecture. Anne Sexton, who was Lowell's student at Boston University before he moved to Harvard, put it this way: "He works with a cold chisel with no more mercy than a dentist. He gets out the decay. But if he is never kind to the poem, he is kind to the poet."

Almost everything about Robert Lowell—"Cal," as I learned to call him as we became friends—cut against the grain of traditional, hidebound Harvard. The contradiction between the Lowell name and Robert Lowell the man puzzled me. Why did he choose, for instance, to have rooms at Quincy House, with its aggressively modern and, to my eye, ugly architecture? Wouldn't he have preferred digs with more character—in Lowell House itself, for example? The choice probably had something to do with his aesthetic sense. Son of an old Boston family, brought up to identify with New England tradition, Lowell rebelled in favor of everything unexpected, shocking, garish. His neckties looked as though they had been bought in a boutique on the Cape. I sometimes wondered whether someone else bought his clothes for him and told him what to wear.

Clearly there was a larger world beyond the concentrated intensity of our little basement room in Quincy House. And just as clearly, Robert Lowell was a citizen of that world. We were vaguely aware that he lived for most of the week in New York—in a Beaux Arts building, as it turned out, next door to the Café des Artistes on West Sixty-seventh Street with his wife, the novelist and critic Elizabeth Hardwick. When I visited him there, he would take me to lunch at a French restaurant near Lincoln Center where the maitre d' fawned appropriately and gave us an excellent table where we addressed ourselves to a pitcher of vodka martinis while studying the menu. When *Hogan's Goat*, by our friend William Alfred, opened at the American Place Theatre in 1965, Lowell's picture appeared on the front page of *Women's Wear Daily* with Jackie Kennedy, whom he had accompanied to the play.

One morning in June of 1965 the *New York Times* printed a letter Lowell wrote to Lyndon Johnson, refusing the president's invitation to the White House Festival of the Arts. "After a week's wondering," he wrote, "I have decided that I am conscience-bound to refuse your courteous invitation." The letter achieves a particularly Lowellian tone, part *cri de coeur*, part socially correct gesture. He goes on to say, "We are in danger of imperceptibly becoming an explosive and suddenly chauvinistic nation, and may even be drifting on our way to the last nuclear ruin." After this evocation of apocalypse, Lowell ends his letter, "At this anguished, delicate and perhaps determining moment, I feel I am serving you and our country best by not taking part in the White House Festival of the Arts."

These events were echoed in our own times when First Lady Laura Bush invited many of the nation's poets to the White House for a day celebrating the poetry of Walt Whitman and Emily Dickinson. Poets organized themselves around a Web site founded by the poet and publisher Sam Hamill and prepared to turn the event into a collective protest against the second Gulf War. The White House promptly canceled the event. How similar the circumstances, how different the flavor of these two eras. Sam Hamill provides the only note of color in the recent brouhaha. Laura Bush, God bless her, wouldn't stand out in a crowd. The president himself didn't even got involved this time around. In the case of Lowell's refusal, by contrast, according to one of LBJ's aides, "The roar in the Oval Office could be heard all the way into the East Wing." Being rejected by Lowell was, for LBJ, one more snub at the hands of the East Coast elite with whom John F. Kennedy had filled the corridors of power. And yet, in "Waking Early Sunday Morning," Lowell saw something of himself in the president from Texas:

> O to break loose. All life's grandeur
> is something with a girl in summer . . .
> elated as the President
> girdled by his establishment
> this Sunday morning, free to chaff
> his own thoughts with his bear-cuffed staff,
> swimming nude, unbuttoned, sick
> of his ghost-written rhetoric!

The idea of serving one's country was important to Robert Traill Spence Lowell IV, whose ancestors came over on the *Mayflower* and whose family had been active in public life, higher education, and military service for over three hundred years. In one of the great political poems of our era, "For the Union Dead," he holds up Colonel Robert Gould Shaw, commander during the Civil War of the black Massachusetts Fifty-fourth, as an example of inspired leadership. As opposed to figures from the contemporary political climate, where "a savage servility / slides by on grease," Colonel Shaw "has an angry wrenlike vigilance, / a greyhound's gentle tautness." Duty motivates him: "He seems to wince at pleasure, / and suffocate for privacy."

He saw these same old-fashioned virtues in the Kennedys. In an elegy for Robert Kennedy, praising his loyalty to his "clan," Lowell movingly wrote, "For them like a prince, you daily left your tower / to walk through dirt in your best cloth."

Two decades earlier the then twenty-six-year-old poet had invoked the same tradition of public service in a letter to President Franklin D. Roosevelt: "I very much regret that I must refuse the opportunity you offer me in your communication of August 6, 1943, for service in the Armed Forces." He sounds as though he were declining an invitation to a dinner party. Closing his letter, he appeals to FDR as one aristocrat to another: "You will understand how painful such a decision is for an American whose family traditions, like your own, have always found their fulfillment in maintaining, through responsible participation in both the civil and the military services, our country's freedom and honor."

In the fall of 1967 he came up to Cambridge for his weekly teaching stint after having participated in the March on Washington the previous weekend. With Dwight Macdonald, Norman Mailer, Noam Chomsky, Dr. Spock, and other notables in attendance, the March represented one of the Left's grandest public occasions, and many extravagant claims were made for what was accomplished there. Firmly opposed to the war as he was, conscious of being a poetic spokesman for the intellectual Left, Lowell was at the same time turned off by what he saw as the self-aggrandizement and self-deception of political rhetoric One of his most bracing strengths was his resistance to cant. He could not buy into the self-dramatization of those he skewered as "standard radicals," who inflated the antiwar movement to the level of the French Revolution. His poem "The March," written immediately after the event, refreshingly and unassumingly puts distance between himself and his fellow demonstrators:

> sadly
> unfit to follow their dream, I sat in the sunset
> shade of their Bastille, the Pentagon,
> nursing leg- and arch-cramps, my cowardly
> foolhardy heart; and heard, alas, more speeches . . .

Underlying the seriousness, the eccentricity, the flair for public gestures, was Lowell's private torment. A victim of what we now call bipolar disorder, he was subject to periodic spells of fantasy-driven fixation and identification with figures from the world of power—from Alexander the Great to Hitler to LBJ. Many of these episodes had their comic side, such as his visit to South America in 1962, when he declared himself "Caesar of Argentina" and told the American cultural attaché, whom he bullied into the position of being his lackey: "I want you to travel with me always. You are my lieutenant."

The world-weariness we at Harvard saw in Lowell no doubt

stemmed from the burden of his illness. These cycles had been occurring since the late 1940s: an upward spiral of manic exhilaration followed by hospitalization and then months spent in the doldrums of a melancholy, vapid numbness. "I keep no rank nor station," he wrote in *Life Studies*. "Cured, I am frizzled, stale and small." Perhaps the worst thing about the depressed state was that he could remember everything he had done and said while "high."

His students have gone on to become distinguished editors and journalists, playwrights, educators, and, of course, poets. The seriousness he brought to the profession of poetry can be seen in the subsequent work of several habitués of his office hours. I wonder whether Alan Williamson and Frank Bidart would have written as well as they have without having apprenticed themselves to a mentor for whom eros and the psyche were obsessions. And the conception of Robert Pinsky's 1979 book, *An Explanation of America,* a masterly series of poems meant to explain American institutions to his young daughter, surely owes something to Robert Lowell, who treated the president of the United States as no more than his equal—and in some cases, his inferior.

Those of us who gathered around Lowell's table at Quincy House did not regard him as the "thoroughbred mental case" of his own self-deprecating characterization in *Life Studies*. Nor, to our credit, I might say, did gossip about his sometimes outrageous behavior hold as much interest for us as it did for some of his biographers. We didn't even waste much time wondering what that babe in the mink coat was doing at Quincy House at 9 A.M.!

His gift to those who studied with him was his example of total dedication to our art. "Writing is rewriting," he would say, and he meant that on the most basic level. To us he was above all else a master poet, and many of us learned the tough-mindedness and perfectionism that go into the lonely discipline of writing from this most ardent, painstaking, and serious man.

# Early and Late

## *Robert Lowell and What Is Real*

Robert Lowell's poems that appeared in the *Kenyon Review* from its first number to its eighth provide a work-in-progress view of his early development. John Crowe Ransom showed high confidence in his protégé's potential by printing two rather jejune poems by the twenty-year-old Kenyon student in volume 1, number 1. These two poems, neither of which was later reprinted in *Lord Weary's Castle,* show several interesting things about the young poet.

One is that, technically, Lowell's particular poetic genius—unlike that of Ransom—did not function well within the narrow confines of the quatrain. His expansive energy expressed itself more naturally in the long verse-paragraphs he learned from *Paradise Lost* and would employ in his masterpiece, "The Quaker Graveyard in Nantucket." His first poem to appear in *Kenyon* (under the name R. T. S. Lowell), "The Cities' Summer Death," begins:

> The summer hospital enframes
> In its fashionable windows
> Boats brow-beaten by vanished storms
> And curbed-off grass where no cows browse.

The off-rhymes—enframes / storms, windows / browse—are odd, perhaps influenced by Ransom's poems or those of Ransom's favorite, Thomas Hardy. The adjective "brow-beaten," odd when applied to boats, shows that Lowell had already discovered the wrenched, idiosyncratic rhetoric that would typify

_____

From the *Kenyon Review.*

his mature style. This rhetoric, represented here only by a compound adjective, carries at least a whiff of violence. A typical later example of it from "Memories of West Street and Lepke," in *Life Studies,* is this description of Mafia enforcers: "Hairy, muscular, suburban, / wearing chocolate double-breasted suits, / they blew their tops and beat him black and blue."

It's hard to tell whether the last line of the quatrain, which blatantly echoes Keats's "La Belle Dame sans Merci"—"The sedge is withered from the Lake / And no birds sing"—is meant to be funny. In any case it shows that Lowell was metrically sophisticated enough to mimic Keats's trick of ending a line with a spondee (almost no other poet does this).

The Classical version of death—Charon ferrying the deceased over the river Styx—appealed to Lowell, who was a classics major at Kenyon. At the same time his imagination was thoroughly grounded in the scenery and folkways of his native Boston. The swan-boats that ply the pond in Boston's Public Garden blended in his mind with Charon's ferry:

> Grandfather feathery as thought
> Furls his flurried wrapper and floats
> Off his adjustable bed
> Wafted on somnolent swan-boats

You can see how carefully Lowell plays with the alliterative f's—a conscious craftsman learning his trade. At the same time that the death of his grandfather—his mentor and surrogate father—must have grieved him, the artist in him works dispassionately—even abstractedly and obscurely, with imagery—in the next quatrain:

> Cancer ossifies his features,
> The starved skeleton shows its teeth,
> Flamingo crackling embroiders
> Italian bones with shameless froth.

What is going on in the last two lines of this stanza? Why are the bones Italian? Why, for that matter, is the poem called "The Cities' Summer Death"? Despite the obscurity, however, the weirdness of imagery and rhetoric may be the most interesting thing about this little poem, showing the Mannerist poet, artistically high-spirited even when bowed down by grief. The last stanza presents the transition from life to death as a grotesque, almost medieval spectacle:

> But the honking untainted swans
> Float over the deathly stream
> And the aghast oarsmen of Charon's
> Ferry raise their skeleton rhythm.

There is a saying, that two things you do not want to see in the making are sausage and legislation. The makings of a distinctive poetic style like that of Lowell in *Lord Weary's Castle* are not necessarily a pretty sight either. This extravagant style brought together at least two kinds of rhetorical excess: an elaborately skewed poetic rhetoric imitating religious poets of the seventeenth century like Richard Crashaw, who specialized in paradox and recherché imagery; and American slang of the 1930s and 1940s. The result, put in the simplest terms, was a blend of high style and low style. When it works it is striking; when it falls short it is embarrassing. "Satan's Confession," from volume 5, number 3, is an example of the latter:

> When providential wit,
> At loggerheads with Sin,
>     Expels this gluttonous fool
>     To hard-knock's School,
> The Hypocrite
> Discovers medicine.

The "gluttonous fool" presumably is Adam. The "little Boy" would be the Christ child:

> Then born, the little Boy
> Bawls in the bestial straw;
>     O Holy Mother strap
>     God to thy pap,
> For this gaunt Toy
> Will suckle Israel's Law!

"I am tired. Everyone's tired of my turmoil," Robert Lowell wrote in his *Life Studies* poem "Eye and Tooth." Lowell was, as readers familiar with his poetry and the several biographies of him are by now all too aware, mentally ill. In the years he has been dead, most of the controversies and injuries caused by his personal turmoil have either been resolved, accepted, or forgotten. It is now possible to look at his idiosyncratic sensibility as expressed in his poetry more in terms of temperament, less in terms of pathology or personal morality.

In *Life Studies* in particular Lowell describes the realities of coping with his bipolar disorder; but typically he does so from the standpoint of someone who is, at least temporarily, cured. The famously downright line in "Skunk Hour," "My mind's not right," is not something a person would say when "crazy." "Enervation" is a key word for Lowell in his depressed, listless condition: "Recuperating, I neither spin nor toil," he writes in "Home after Three Months Away," ending the poem on this low note: "I keep no rank nor station. / Cured, I am frizzled, stale and small."

As I pointed out in my critical memoir, *Robert Lowell's Life and Work: Damaged Grandeur,* one reason Lowell made the shift from rhyme and meter to free verse (or "prose" as he sometimes called it) was that he associated rhyme and meter with madness, free verse with sobriety and sanity. Readers have tended to misunderstand the meaning of this change for Lowell because it runs counter to what the transition from so-called "form" to "free verse" meant to most poets in the 1960s, during the popularity of the anthology *Naked Poetry,* when it was common to use the highly freighted terms "open form" and "closed form," with the built-in connotations of the words "open" and "closed." Free verse to poets like Bly, Kinnell, Wright, and Rich meant expansion and liberation, letting themselves get loose. To Lowell it meant self-limitation, "behaving," pulling in his horns.

Robert Hass was among the first to see how in the *Naked Poetry* climate of opinion a neatly schematic but muddle-headed version of Lowell's development became the one that most readers unthinkingly nodded assent to:

I still find myself blinking incredulously when I read—in almost anything written about the poetry—that those early poems "clearly reflect the dictates of the new criticism," while the later ones are "less consciously wrought and extremely intimate." This is the view in which it is "more intimate" and "less conscious" to say "my mind's not right" than to imagine the moment when

> The death-lance churns into the sanctuary, tears
> The gun-blue swingle, heaving like a flail,
> And hacks the coiling life out . . .

which is to get things appallingly wrong.
("Lowell's Graveyard," from *Twentieth Century Pleasures*)

Trying to become cured, to achieve psychic salvation, Lowell quite deliberately tried to put the mania of his early genius behind him. The result was a dual tragedy. Not only did the cure ultimately not take. One could in addition make the claim that the loss of this radical, mad vision was the tragedy of Lowell's life as a poet. The depth of his dilemma—that he could only be cured by giving up what was most essential to who he was—was not clear to many of us during the *Life Studies* and *For the Union Dead* period. For one thing, when doctors first began giving him lithium to control his disorder, the cure at first appeared to be working. For another, in *Life Studies* he seemed, during the heyday of Confessional poetry, to be doing his best work—though for many readers the clarity of *Life Studies* did not make up for the lost fire of "The Quaker Graveyard."

Once he gave up the public, clarifying mission of *Life Studies, For the Union Dead,* and *Near the Ocean,* he indulged himself again during the last ten years of his life, in introspection—this time more truly personal though less sensational than what he had written about in his Confessional period. Here are a few lines from "Double-Vision" in *The Dolphin,* published four years before his death:

> The cat walks out—
> or does it? The room has filled with double-shadows,
> sedation doubles everything I see . . .

You can't be here, and yet we try to talk;
Somebody else is farcing in your face . . .


The positive side of Lowell's mania is the weird brilliance he
brought to his writing both toward the end of his career and in
the years before his illness had actually been diagnosed and he
began to feel that the dangerous energy of his poetry boiled in
the same pot that poisoned his grip on reality. The early poem
"Winter in Dunbarton" seethes with a conviction that there is
something terribly wrong with the world. Time and death, the
poem says, are the major flaws. But the poet widens his net to
ensnare the New England heritage which he so thoroughly ex-
coriates in his early work. And his father plays an ambivalent
role. The poem is sufficiently complex, as are the changes Lowell made in it before reprinting it in *Lord Weary's Castle,* that I really should quote it in its entirety:


### Winter in Dunbarton

Time smiling on this sundial of a world
Corrupted the snow-monster and the worm,
Ransacker of shard statues and the peers
Of Europe; but our cat is cold, is curled
For rigor mortis: she no longer smears
Her catnip mouse from Christmas; the germ,
Mindless and ice, a world against our world,
Hurtles her round of brains into her ears;

This winter only snowmen turn to stone:
And, sick of the long hurly-burly, rise
Like butterflies into Jehovah's eyes
And shift until their crystals must atone

To water; but the days are short and rot
The holly on our Father's mound. All day
The wastes of snow about my house stare in
Through idle windows at the brainless cat;
The coke-barrel in the corner whimpers. May
The snow recede and red clay furrows set
In the grim grin of their erosion, in
The fusion of uprooted fallow, fat

With muck and winter dropsy, where the tall
Snow-monster wipes the coke-fumes from his eyes
And scatters his corruption and it lies
Gaping until the fungus-eyeballs fall

Into this eldest of the seasons. Cold
Cracks the bronze toes and fingers of the Christ
Our Father fetched from Florence, and the dead
Narrow to nothing in the thankless ground
Grandfather wrenched from Charlie Stark and sold
To the selectmen of Dunbarton. Head
And shoulders narrow; Father's stone is crowned
With snowflakes and the bronze-age shards of Christ.

To observe that this poem reflects a very dire and strange state of mind, and that its logic poses extreme challenges, is not very astute criticism; but this observation is probably the first any reader is likely to make. The world is a sundial; yet the two figures that represent it are the "snow-monster" (altered to "snowman" in *Lord Weary's Castle*) and the worm. Since the worm of mortality would normally be seen as an agent of corruption, it's odd that "smiling" Time corrupts the corrupter. The world in this view is a battleground of mutual predation. The worm is "Ransacker of shard statues and the peers / Of Europe" (the first part of this characterization gets changed to "Sacker of painted idols," which doesn't change the sense of it very much), but only after being corrupted by time. The point about time, then, must be understood as theological: the world changed from "sundial" to a scene of corruption and conflict at the Fall of Man.

Having touched lightly on the poem's logical argument—and admittedly the authority of Lowell's voice derives partially from the power of his intellect—what I want to do here is put the poem's logic on hold and address its mood or atmosphere. This is, to me, more interesting, because it gives us a closer look into Lowell's inner world and allows us to appreciate the strange beauty of it rather than seeing it, in the terms I have outlined above, as a form of pathology.

The intensity of existential bleakness in some of Lowell's poetry is almost unique to him. It perhaps reaches its peak mid-career in the title poem of *Near the Ocean,* where degradation and squalor are presented with something like glee:

> Some subway-green coldwater flat,
> its walls tattooed with neon light,
> then high delirious squalor, food
> burned down with vodka . . . menstrual blood
> caking the covers, when they woke
> to the dry, childless Sunday walk,
> saw cars on Brooklyn Bridge descend
> through steel and coal dust to land's end.

That stanza presents the bleakness as something in the lives of two people. Then he takes the two out for a walk on the shore. For him the ocean—which, "grinding stones, / can only speak the present tense"—represents what he sees as the cold, elemental brutality of existence:

> Is it this shore? Their eyes worn white
> as moons from hitting bottom? Night,
> the sandfleas scissoring their feet,
> the sandbed cooling to concrete,
> one borrowed blanket, lights of cars
> shining down at them like stars?
> Sand built the lost Atlantis . . . sand,
> Atlantic Ocean, condoms, sand.

In "The Quaker Graveyard in Nantucket," twenty years before he wrote "Near the Ocean," the ocean was already a powerful icon for him, but it was mythic and colorful, seen as a living being, not as the blank stare of an uncaring life-force in the face of which human existence was meaningless. Here he addresses the sailors:

> When you are powerless
> To sand-bag this Atlantic bulwark, faced
> By the earth-shaker, green, unwearied, chaste,
> In his steel scales; ask for no Orphean lute
> To pluck life back . . .

This way of thinking about the ocean is altogether more heroic and life-infused than the understanding he had come to after twenty years of breakdown, treatment, and cures that were almost worse than the illness they were designed to correct.

I have digressed to how Lowell grappled with the macrocosm, the ocean as its emblem. "Winter in Dunbarton" inclines more toward the microcosm. From a mention of "the peers of Europe" the focus narrows domestically to the dying cat, "curled / For rigor mortis." The germ which has attacked it, at the bottom of existence, takes on the power of "a world against our world." The remarkable thing about this poem is how fixated it is on corruption and death. The atmosphere is all desolation: "All day / The wastes of snow about my house stare in / Through idle windows at the brainless cat . . ." Even the hope of spring is grim: "May / The snow recede and red clay furrows set / In the grim grin of their erosion . . ."

The *Kenyon Review* version appears to anticipate Lowell's father's death by a decade: "the days are short and rot / The holly on our Father's mound." When he revised the poem for *Lord Weary's Castle,* he withdrew that wish and changed the line to read, "Belle, the cat that used to rat / About my father's books, is dead." Still, in the last stanza, he returns to the statue of Christ "Our Father fetched from Florence" (revised to "My father fetched from Florence"). The ending is ambiguous, but firmly focused on death and devoid of any hope one might expect to derive from religious faith: "Father's stone is crowned / With snowflakes and the bronze-age shards of Christ." Christ here would seem to be ancient, but just as subject to corruption and disintegration as everything else in the grim, wintry world.

Even in the long sequence *History,* from 1973, with its declared public theme, Lowell's impulse was to turn inside, to see figures like Stalin and Robin Hood as if they were versions of himself. It must have become clear to him that what he calls "my old infection" would be with him the rest of the way. Often content to range no more widely than the limits of his own psyche, he precisely delineates his condition in "Symptoms":

> A dog seems to lap water from the pipes,
> a wheeze of dogsmell and dogcompanionship—

life-enhancing water brims my bath—
(the bag of waters or the lake of the grave . . . ?)
from the palms of my feet to my wet neck—
I have no mother to lift me in her arms.
I feel my old infection, it comes once yearly:
lowered good humor, then an ominous
rise of irritable enthusiasm . . .

As in "The Quaker Graveyard" and "Near the Ocean" the element water still excites his imagination, but here it is closer, more intimate: bath water, the amniotic fluid, and what he foresaw as "the lake of the grave."

Writing to Allen Tate from Kenyon while Lowell was still a student there, John Crowe Ransom called him at the time he was writing the early poems under consideration here, "a fine boy, very definitely with great literary possibilities." Like other artists of great ambition and scope, Lowell at an early age was trying out different styles which while failing almost laughably at the time, would lead later to the achievement of a mature style. And even given the exaggerations and excesses of these early poems, Lowell announces himself to be the poet whom Peter Viereck would describe soon after as "best qualified to restore to our literature its sense of the tragic and the lofty."

# Travel and the Sense of Place

Southern writers are sometimes asked to explain something called "the sense of place." This quasi-mystical sense is transmitted at birth—so I am told—to every writer from the Faulkner Belt, moist with mother's milk and holy water, like that other supposed birthright, the ability to tell a good story. If I had a dollar for every time I have been asked why Southerners possess the narrative gift, I could quit my job in the North and retire to that mythic homestead, the Family Plantation. I have stashed the deed to it in the same attic trunk where I keep my Confederate money.

This particular prejudice about Southern writers—friendly, but a prejudice nonetheless—always surprises me because it implies that fiction writers and poets from other parts of the country somehow lack a sense of place. I was gratified to see my contemporary Robert Pinsky describe himself, in *The Best American Poetry 1992*, as having been "born in the historic seaside resort town of Long Branch, New Jersey," suggesting that you don't have to be Southern to acknowledge where you come from.

It seems odd to single out the sense of place as a distinctive value because, after all, the world is a place. It is a place that contains other places: The stubble fields of Haywood County, Tennessee, where I shot quail as a boy. The dusty grounds of Sancta Sophia in Istanbul, where I have passed happy afternoons poking around among fragments of Greek statuary and columns from the fifth century. The Irish fishing village of Kinvara on Galway Bay, with its nine pubs and its maritime skies, where I spend part of each year.

The world is a place. Some writers, perhaps the greatest, have

From *Poetry Ireland Review.*

taken a particular place and made it a Globe Theatre, the stage for action of universal import. William Faulkner famously wrote, "I discovered that my own little postage stamp of native soil was worth writing about and that I would never live long enough to exhaust it." This apotheosis of the local gave confidence to a generation of Southern writers. Patrick Kavanagh encouraged a kindred rootedness among Irish writers: "To know fully even one field or one lane is a lifetime's experience . . . A gap in a hedge, a smooth rock surfacing a narrow lane, a view of a woody meadow, the stream at the junction of four small fields—these are as much as a man can fully experience."

Plenitude may be found anywhere, then—though, tragically, a place can be destroyed spiritually, and become a non-place. Attunement to a variety of places rather than to one native or chosen place is what characterizes the writer who drinks from many wells, who sometimes feels more at home when he is in a foreign place. As I glance at the poems I have taped up on the walls of the room where I sit, I am spirited back to several places, each with its own history, quality of light, kind of dirt, birds and trees, its own currency and savor.

To say that place is the Muse in her several guises is no more fanciful than to believe with the ancient Greeks, American Indians, or other pre-monotheistic peoples that each river, mountain, or canyon is inhabited by its own genius loci. Czeslaw Milosz writes in his *ABC's,* "Every river has its own soul, which is revealed when we stand on its banks." Wordsworth invokes his Presences,

> Ye powers of earth, ye genii of the springs,
> And ye that have your voices in the clouds,
> And ye that are familiars of the lakes
> And of the standing pools

and he is not, in my view, speaking conventionally or metaphorically, indulging himself in what we were taught in school to regard as the rhetorical device of personification. Wordsworth's invocation is an instance of the attuned poet's deliberate communication with the spirits of place.

These spirits are not always welcomers or nourishers: they may assert themselves against the poet's will, as happens in Seamus Heaney's "Bog Oak" to Edmund Spenser, who while "dreaming sunlight" in Ireland, where he served as a colonial administrator, finds himself "encroached upon" by

> geniuses who creep
> "out of every corner
> of the woodes and glennes"
> towards watercress and carrion.

When I look at my own poems taped along the walls, the farm in Haywood County comes back to dazzle my mind's senses with the saturated yellow of homely ragweed seen at dawn, the earthy must of the nineteenth-century white clapboard farmhouse built right down on the ground, the sting of iron in water pumped ice-cold out of the well and kept in a cedar bucket hanging on the back porch, or the delicate gonging of a chipped enamel wash basin when banged against the edge of a wooden table. Interlacing these impressions are "a boy's brainy and indolent imaginings," as one of my poems has it.

### Firstness

Early pleasures please best, some old voice whispers:
Cozy holdings, the heart's iambic thud
And sly wanderings—lip-touchings, long summers,
The rain's pourings and pipings heard from bed;
Earth-smell of old houses, airy ceilings,
A boy's brainy and indolent imaginings.

Twenty years gone then that boy is gone,
Speeding down beach roads in a friend's MG.
Love, or the limey buzz of a g'n't—
Or better, both—and the watery hunter's moon,
Accelerate the engines of the night,
And set a long chase afoot.

Today, twenty years older than that even,
I breathe quietness and fresh-laundered linen,
Kneeling, seeing with eyes opened white brick,
Smelling Sunday, mumbling beside my son those words
About a lost sheep, and someone's having erred.
Thank God for instinct, and beginner's luck.

Here's another poem from that same place:

*Allen's Station: They*
*for Beverly Travers*

The stars cool their fires in the river of night.
The big people sleep.
I step out barefooted onto the dewy, rough-boarded porch
And open my eyes among farm buildings.
Their yellow pine boards and whitewash
Illuminate my way.

Down the kitchen-garden path, through the orchard,
All the way this side of the leaning barn
Where the horses shuffle and snore,
Past a slumbering bull in a meadow,
Past the for-once quiet chickens

I pad over velvet dust,
Through heady stands of ragweed,
Past the cooks' cabin
Where Kate and Aunt Martha
Have lit the morning lamp already
In their sturdy square cabin
Wallpapered with years of the Sunday comics.

Orphan Annie's eyes
Never narrow or squint
Like Aunt Martha's do
And Dick Tracy is forever in profile
And will never look straight at lame, hobbled Martha
Who was born a slave
And because even her church is on the property,
Has never left these acres.

And red-headed, Cherokee Kate
Who never has a civil word for no one
But my Uncle Frank—Why is that, I wonder?—
A different kind of uncle;
A cousin more like, if the tree were drawn.

Dagwood blunders across these walls
And will do so in his Bumstead way
Until the paper peels.

And Blondie with her 'thirties frizz
Is out shopping again
And will again commit the crime of unthrift;
And Major Hoople in his quilted dressing-gown harrumphs,
Fires up his meerschaum pipe
And sums up his opinion of life at Allen's Station:
"Egad!"

George A. and his wife and her sister and her sister's husband
And their three children, and Napoleon,
And a walleyed Indian-looking woman with a corncob pipe,
And some people I don't recognize
Are going to the fields today to chop cotton.

Their blue overalls bleached to the ghost of white,
Their streaming Mason jars of well water,
Their readiness for whatever reason to work twelve hours
In the West Tennessee sun—
People today don't look like them, or talk like them.

The whites of Napoleon's eyes are purple.
Later in the morning, when he feels a little better,
He'll tell me again about the penitentiary
And show me the healed, pink bullet hole in his arm.

I'm seven, the farmer's little cousin from Memphis.

The lug-wheeled John Deere tractor
Strains with its wagonload of people
And follows the sun up and over the raised L&N tracks
That divide our farm from Beverly's father's.

The land surrounds us with its life:
Not the soil only—the oaks and poplars and sycamores
And cotton plants and birds and beasts,
And all of us a part of it:
The people who work it, the farmer who owns it,
The boy who watches.

At the end of August my uncle
Will flag down the L&N
And I'll ride it to Memphis
Through the whitewashed towns and sparse farms
And be met in a car
At the big station built with cotton dollars,
And go back to school
And grow up and move away.

They stay in the fields.
I watch them chop cotton,
Drinking water from their jar—
And them not seeming to mind—

As the dense green cotton leaves burn
And the purple boll explodes into ripeness
And the sun describes its slow arc.

They chop cotton, and stay right where they are.


Istanbul is a sky half Mediterranean, half Balkan, smudged
with coalsmoke, diesel exhaust, and the succulence of roasting
lamb. Permeating the atmosphere of the present, a traveler
who knows his Ottoman history feels the strained hauteur of
vanished empire. The ground in mosque-yards buckles under
tombstones—marble shafts surmounted by stylized turbans,
where grandees of the *ancien régime* decay, their markers half
toppled by neglect and the passage of time, strangled with
brambles.


### Pasha's Daughter, 1918

Braided into a single complication
Down the back of her nightdress, her hair shows grey
As pearls and white as a cloud as she steps coldly
To open the curtains' plum velvet, stiff with thread of silver,
Onto a sky above Istanbul. Mehmet brings *chai*
On a silver tray worn through to copper.

A Jerusalem cypress in her garden
That arrows the sky as a minaret does—
Its lines liquid as a page of Persian—
A leaded mosque-dome full and silvery in the pause
Between showers, give her the sense of having awakened
And been served tea in Paradise.

Paradise is a bedraggled trapezoid
Of outback, its fountain a brew of leaves,
Its marble paths dog-fouled. The Black Sea wind blows
Trash against untended tulips gone to seed.
Rain storms and gutters down the overarching eaves
And rattles the quiet of her windows.

Tarnished stars invisible above Istanbul
Govern, while trains from Aleppo and the Balkans
Shuttle broken armies home to the capital.
The ground buckles under tombstones. Marble turbans
Crack, as the bones of the ancients are shoveled aside
To make space for the freshly dead.

Mehmet comes in again, six centuries
Of marches and conquests reduced to the dirt
On his cuffs. Moustache dispirited, nomadic cheekbones
Wintry, he lights a fire, smudging the famous skies
With coal scavenged from the cobbled street.
Her eyes would break bones.

Thunder now—like the clatter of musketry,
Like war ponies galloped across borders,
Like bronze siege-cannon pounding Viennese stone,
Like the voice of a shattered gong the circumference of the
    sky.
"Bring opium to me by the window," she orders,
"While I watch our empire melt in the rain."


Kinvara: The smell of a turf fire, sleet rattling the window
panes, the broad-shouldered gravity of two- and three-story
limestone row houses asserting the land's claim against gales
that thrust in off the Atlantic. For a moment or two I am back
in my writing room there in County Galway, looking out a west
window streaked with rain, over limestone-walled pasture land
where sheep graze, up toward the mountains of Clare.
   Here is "A Quiet Pint in Kinvara":


### A Quiet Pint in Kinvara

Salt-stung, rain-cleared air, deepened as always
By a smudge of turf smoke. Overhead the white glide
Of seagulls, and in the convent beeches above the road,
Hoarse croak of rooks, throaty chatter of jackdaws.
High tide pounds stone wall.
I shut the door behind me and head downhill,

Gait steadied by the broad-shouldered gravity
Of houses from the eighteenth or nineteenth century—
Limestone, three storeys, their slate roofs rain-slick,

Aglow with creeper and the green brilliance of mosses.
No force off the Atlantic
Could threaten their angles or budge their masses.

They rise unhurriedly from the strong cellar
And hold a fleshy hand, palm outward, against the sea,
Saying "Land starts here. Go peddle your salt airs elsewhere."
From farms down lanes the meat and milk of pasture,
Root crops and loads of hay,
By hoof or wagon, come down to Kinvara quay.

And so do I—to drink in the presence
Of these presences, these ideas given substance,
Solid as your father's signature
On a letter you unfold sometimes from a quiet drawer,
Yet semi-detached, half free,
Like the road that follows the sea down from Galway,

Curving like a decorated S
Drizzled through a monk's quill plucked from the goose,
Spelling Sanctus onto vellum newly missed by the herd,
In a cell where the soul's damp candle flared—
Roofless now to the weather's
Inundations, while ravens walk the cloisters.

Gloria of martyrdom, kingship's crimson
Are shattered now, buried in mire. The mizzling sky
Darkens unmitigated over thatch collapsed in the famine,
Tracks leading nowhere. Absences occupy
The four kingdoms. A wide-eyed
Angel stares uncomprehendingly skyward,

Stone angel of the Island, baptised by rain,
Outlasting Viking longboat, Norman strongbow,
Face battered by a rifle butt. Tough-minded as a bloody saint.
But where was I off to, mind like a darkened window
This dampened afternoon?
To the pub of course. It's time for that quiet pint,

Brewed blacker than ruination, sound
As fresh-hewn timber, strong as a stonecutter's hand.
Make it stout like the roof overhead, to take off the chill
That blows through emptied fields. Let me drink my fill
And more, of that architecture—
Then ease home tight and respectable to dinner.

Each of these places has something important to say about the human spirit, something I am scanting here. Without it, of course, the evocation of sense impressions counts for little. Attunement to place relates to what Keats called Negative Capability. The traveler squatting on his heels in the back seat of a bus braving the mountainous overnight run from Istanbul to Trebizond, having reduced his impedimenta to the minimum—a canvas bag with reliable straps, a bottle of water with pine trees stenciled on the glass, a change of clothes, the stiff, expatriate dollars in his wallet uncomfortable alongside the gaudy local bills.

### Anatolian Journey

Impedimenta of the self
Left behind somewhere, or traded
For a bag with good straps, a book of Turkish proverbs,
Sandals of proven leather,
A bottle of water called, yes, "Life"
In the language of the country—pine trees
            stencilled on the glass.

Last Thursday you were standing by a puddle
            in Istanbul asking a question:
"Why am I not home, where I should be?"
Now you're east into Asia, hearing absently
            alien conjugations,
Hoping this bus won't dizzy off this mountain.

        "So you think you're a fish now?"
        "It's true that time is a river."
From dreaming fingers your rings dumbly witness your
    travels.
One hand goes to your wallet, where sober dollars
        stiffly face the gaudy local bills.
Your passport is there as well,
                establishing your identity.

        Nod, and in the morning wake to
Acres of sunflowers
                warmer than any human welcome;
Haystacks domed like the domes of whitewashed mosques,
        And the Black Sea rising out of itself
                like the fragrance of remoteness.

This traveler, who understands despite his best efforts perhaps one word in ten of the desultory conversation proceeding sleepily around him, provides an emblem of "the invisible poet" moving through the world. This sojourner in foreign parts wishes above almost everything else to mingle with his fellow passengers, or with the pilgrims at the Burning Ghats on the banks of the Ganges in Benares, let's say, or the Irish farmers at P. J. Flatley's pub in Kinvara, without spoiling the natural flow of things with his presence. It's an absorption almost impossible to manage, but moments do arrive when protective coloration avails, and the "locals" forget you are there, or briefly fail to notice that you are not one of them. (Perhaps at such moments you do become one of them.)

### The Winter Funerals

The postman totters up our street. He's late
Or early, like spring, or he doesn't come at all.
You practice your violin, I go for a stroll
And watch the oysterman tarring his boat
That the storm stove in—the rough weather that brought
The lines down that night after New Year's
When the farmers' faces ran with tears
Outside the house where Mary Flatley was laid out.

We've brushed our black clothes off and put them away.
Someone is cooking, someone's out tending the stock
In the grainy drizzle that settles the turf smoke.
Obscured up there in the weathered sky,
The wind that troubled our winter still blows above
The village. We drink it at night with our whiskey
And stir it into our morning tea,
Hearing the tune Charlie played over Maggie's grave.

That drowsy reel's feet danced in the new-dug mud
Of the grave, and held its drained face up to the rain
When he played it slow on his dark accordion—
That grievous dance step Charlie played.
It follows me out this morning up and down
As I buy a stamp or run an errand
And go for a pint at Flatley's tavern,
Where Mary's smile is nowhere to be seen.

Nowhere in the pipesmoke and mirrored coolness
Where she heard the farmers' chaff with a tolerant ear.
Nowhere to be seen but present everywhere
Amid the slow talk and the Guinness.
Her smile followed the gossip—predictable
As the stuffed pheasants in their glass cases,
Old as the posters for the Galway races.
She gave a love that was almost invisible—

Like the voice at the foot of the garden, the thorny warble
I hear when I get home and pull on my boots
And squelch out among the cabbages and beets
To spot that spring voice, invisible
Or nearly so, that weightless, redbreasted, sparse-feathered
Heartbeat that lilts in the battered garden,
That sings its song for no sound reason
And dies among the thorns unheralded.

You practice your music, I sniff the wind for a sign,
While down in the mud the cabbages glow
With a green persistence. All day you play
That tune, that same old tune, till it's right as rain.


Participation in the larger currents of life means more to me
than any attempt I might make to produce a self-portrait. Why?
For one thing, the Confessional poets have left a bad taste in
our mouths, a bad taste with, in the language of wine, a "long
finish." Despite my admiration for Robert Lowell's poetry, I still
cannot disagree with his own statement: "I am tired, everyone's
tired, of my turmoil." As for Sylvia Plath, even years later it is
hard to wash the smell of death from one's nostrils.

The Confessional poets pose an example of the writer in ex-
tremis, under a bell jar, too wrapped up in the self to look outside. Travel is one way among many to get out of oneself—a geographical metaphor for psychic adventure. Lowell uses an
implied metaphor of place in his agonized poem "Skunk Hour":
"I myself am hell; / nobody's here." Interestingly, in one of Elizabeth Hardwick's letters to him that Lowell quotes in *The Dolphin,* she invokes a foreign culture in urging him teasingly to
emerge from his self-absorption: "Why don't you lose yourself /
and write a play about the fall of Japan?"

It must be admitted, though, that the poet as traveler is the poet as observer, the one who does not quite belong. Is travel a substitute for the spiritual journey of the imagination? Elizabeth Bishop, in her brilliant poem "Questions of Travel," poses this question, only to complicate it further: "Is it lack of imagination that makes us come / to imagined places, not just stay at home?" Home is a preoccupation of American poets, no doubt because so many of us leave home—though home is not the given commodity it is often taken to be. Elizabeth Bishop puts an even further twist on her own question by answering it with another: "Should we have stayed at home, / wherever that may be?"

# W. B. Yeats

## *The Labyrinth of Another's Being*

The veils surrounding William Butler Yeats come in such degrees of thickness and coloration that we shall probably never see the man plain. The title of one of the first major critical studies, *Yeats: The Man and the Masks,* by Richard Ellmann, addressed the questions of disguise and shifting identities—questions that have continued to engage commentators. Yeats's early work planted so persuasively in readers' minds a picture of the dreamer swathed in the mists of the Celtic Twilight that the conflicting reality of him as a man of the world, shrewd man of business, keenly aware of cash flow and reputation, has come as a surprise and even a betrayal of some readers' images of him. Yeats went to his grave a convinced occultist and believer in the spirit world. Recent biography reveals that this mystic was also skillful at self-promotion, an experienced committee man, trenchant debater, and politician—not to mention a fierce competitor at croquet.

All this is complicated even further by Yeats's reinvention of himself in the early years of Modernism, producing a flowering of mature poetry probably unequaled since the late plays of Shakespeare. In retrospect, because of our high valuation of Yeats's later poetry, it is hard to grasp that for Yeats's contemporaries at the outbreak of the first World War, he seemed a man whose best work was already behind him. The tendency among American readers to view all things Irish through a

Review of *W. B. Yeats: The Man and the Milieu,* by Keith Alldritt (New York: Clarkson Potter, 1997) and *W. B. Yeats: A Life, I: The Apprentice Mage, 1865–1914,* by R. F. Foster (Oxford: Oxford University Press, 1997). From the *New Criterion.*

green veil of sentimentality—a tendency Yeats himself played along with—is another obstacle to clear vision. Perhaps no life can be thoroughly understood, but the student of this great poet finds himself especially awed by the complex task of entering into what Yeats called "the labyrinth of another's being." In this essay I intend to concentrate on Yeats's first fifty years.

G. K. Chesterton, who encountered him wearing a top hat and carrying binoculars at the Dublin Horse Show in the early 1920s, was amazed by how much the supposedly otherworldly poet knew about horseflesh and handicapping. But such knowledge would have come naturally to Yeats, who as a young man lived in Sligo with his uncle George Pollexfen:

> In muscular youth well known to Mayo men
> For horsemanship at meets or at racecourses,
> That could have shown how pure-bred horses
> And solid men, for all their passion, live
> But as the outrageous stars incline
> By opposition, square and trine . . .
>             ("In Memory of Major Robert Gregory")

His Uncle George was a convert to Yeats's belief in astrology and, like his nephew, evidently found nothing contradictory about parallel interests in the stars and the turf. Perhaps the ostensible contradiction lies less in Yeats's prismatic self than in our own ideas about what constitutes an integrated personality.

A story often told, usually with an air of mildly scandalized amusement over pints of Guinness in Dublin's literary pubs, involves Yeats's reaction to being informed over the telephone by *Irish Times* editor Bertie Smyllie that he had won the Nobel Prize for Literature in 1923. "Yeats halted the journalist's flow," as Keith Alldritt recounts the tale in his new biography, *W. B. Yeats: The Man and the Milieu*, "with a short, practical question. 'How much, Smyllie, how much is it?' The answer was 7,000 pounds."

What the Irish call begrudgery is pandemic in the Dublin literary world, and no writer's success has been more grudgingly acknowledged by his compatriots—during his own time and continuing into the present—than Yeats's. In the "How much is it?" anecdote Yeats figures as a hypocrite: the air of Parnassus is supposed to be unadulterated by the smell of money. The first volume of R. F. Foster's monumental *W. B. Yeats: A Life,* however, reveals for the first time the poverty of Yeats's youth. As an adult he kept a sharp eye on the pounds, shillings, and pence because life under the rented and frequently shifting roof provided in London or Dublin by his father, the artist John B. Yeats, had been precarious and humiliating. In an age of agents, publishers, and book deals, it is easy to overlook the importance of patronage in the writing lives of the great Modernists: "In literary history Augusta Gregory's enduring support of Yeats compares in importance with that given to James Joyce by Harriet Shaw Weaver. Modernist literature was in considerable part a literature of patronage rather than of the market-place." This useful insight may partially explain the willful obscurity often encountered in Modernist works.

Other aspects of *fin de siècle* and early twentieth-century life are easy to lose sight of. Shortly before Yeats's arrival in Paris during the 1890s, when he first met Synge and helped steer him toward the Aran Islands, where the young playwright would discover his true subjects, there were large demonstrations led by the Socialists. In 1893 the anarchist Vaillant hurled a bomb into the Chamber of Deputies, and Captain Dreyfus was court-martialed the same year. The ultra-nationalism and anti-semitism of the Dreyfus period help us understand the political orientation of Yeats's beloved Maud Gonne, who was carrying on a long affair with the right-wing French politician Lucien Millevoye.

Here is Yeats in Dublin just after winning the Nobel Prize and buying a large Georgian house in Merrion Square, one of Dublin's most impressive addresses: "As a host Yeats dressed the part of the world-famous poet. He wore a black velvet coat and silver buckled shoes, a wide black ribbon attached to his tortoiseshell rimmed glasses. On his little finger he wore a large ring of gold. One of his guests was Sean O'Casey, a gauche, prickly little man wearing a cloth cap and steel-rimmed glasses who had grown up in the poorer neighborhoods in Dublin."

Looking back in his autobiographical book, *Reveries over Childhood and Youth,* Yeats in his late forties drew a veil over his painfully threadbare years as an unsuccessful artist's son in London and Dublin, preferring to dwell on carefree days spent in Sligo with his mother's family, the Pollexfens, wealthy merchants and ship-owners. His father's people, the Yeatses, had a distinguished history but, in common with other members of the Protestant establishment or Ascendancy, had come down in the world as a result of the famine, land agitation, and immigration which deprived the *rentier* class of their incomes during the mid–nineteenth century.

Yeats's romantic view of imperiled aristocracy was fed in his youth by sojourns at Sandymount Castle, a turreted and castellated Gothic mansion in the suburbs of Dublin. Here they rode to hounds and drank out of silver cups; Yeats's sister Lily would remember an older relative who "had a most impressive way of dropping his voice and saying sadly, 'so very sad that so and so had to be sold.'" The Yeatses, linen merchants from Yorkshire, had come over to Dublin in the early eighteenth century. In 1773 one Benjamin Yeats married Mary Butler, from the distinguished family of the Dukes of Ormonde, among the most powerful Anglo-Norman families in Ireland. The Yeatses were proud of their Ormonde connection and used Butler as a middle name for the next two centuries.

Yeats's mother's family derived from a less aristocratic lineage and were less caught up in regretting a vanished, partially fictional past. Unlike the Yeatses, they had the advantage of being rich: "The house was so big that there was always a room to hide in, and I had a red pony and a garden where I could wander, and there were two dogs to follow at my heels, one white with some black spots on his head and the other with long black hair all over him." The details of the two dogs are characteristic of Yeats's descriptive writing—always vivid but not necessarily going in any perceptible direction. His writing is wonderfully succinct and concrete, always with an eye to vigorous action.

Of his grandfather William Pollexfen he writes: "He had a violent temper and kept a hatchet at his bedside for burglars and would knock a man down instead of going to law, and I once saw him hunt a party of men with a horsewhip." Mr. Pollexfen may have been "in trade" and thus excluded from houses like Lissadell and Coole where Yeats would later be welcomed; but in his grandson's eyes he had all the virtues of the landed gentry. Thus a strong poet like Yeats not only reinvented himself but even went back and reinvented his past.

Decisive, cleanly defined action is the meat and drink of Yeats's poetry. He associated it with a tradition growing out of the Middle Ages, a way of life whose mainstays were the aristocracy and the peasantry. A vigorous set of values centered around personal courage, sound workmanship, and pride has been his legacy not only to the Irish poets he addressed a month or two before his death in "Under Ben Bulben," but to a century of English-speaking poets who have apprenticed themselves to him:

> Irish poets, learn your trade,
> Sing whatever is well made,
> Scorn the sort now growing up
> All out of shape from toe to top,
> Their unremembering hearts and heads
> Base-born products of base beds.
> Sing the peasantry, and then
> Hard-riding country gentlemen . . .

Yeats's pride in ancestry, his scorn of anything common, made him anathema to critics on the Left, who have of course dominated the intellectual life of the twentieth century.

John B. Yeats, a Trinity College graduate and barrister who gave up the law just two years after the birth of his eldest son in order to study art, was as Foster puts it, "an unVictorian father" who wrote his wife during one of their frequent separations, "Working and caring for children makes me anxious and careful of them, but amusing them makes me fond of them." As inept as he was at supporting his children, and lacking the means to send them to good schools, he nevertheless provided them with an incomparable education for leading the artistic lives they were to lead: W. B. Yeats in poetry, Jack B. Yeats as a painter whose canvases fetch higher and higher prices every year, and the sisters "Lily" and "Lolly" as printers, book designers, weavers, and craftswomen.

When Yeats was in his mid-teens the family moved back to Ireland from London, to live near Dublin in Howth, then a picturesque fishing village. At the age of fifteen or sixteen he began to compose verses. In *Reveries over Childhood and Youth,* creating atmosphere with broad descriptive strokes, he writes, "My father's influence upon my thoughts was at its height. We went to Dublin by train every morning, breakfasting at his studio. He had taken a large room with a beautiful eighteenth-century mantelpiece in a York Street tenement-house, and at breakfast he read passages from the poets, and always from the play or poem at its most passionate moment." It is typical of Yeats's approach that the "beautiful eighteenth-century mantelpiece" somehow dominates the mood of the passage. What is striking is that the obscure and unsuccessful portrait painter John B. Yeats's aesthetic would become the prevailing aesthetic of Modernist poetry: "He never read me a passage because of its speculative interest, and indeed did not care at all for poetry where there was generalization or abstraction however impassioned." Think of the Victorian poetry that was then in vogue and you will see how radical these ideas were at the time.

He fostered in his son a conviction that the best poetry is always personal and dramatic: "He did not care even for a fine lyric passage unless he felt some actual man behind its elaboration of beauty . . . He thought Keats a greater poet than Shelley, because less abstract, but did not read him, caring little, I think, for any of that most beautiful poetry which has come in modern times from the influence of painting. All must be an idealization of speech, and at some moment of passionate action or somnambulistic reverie."

John B. Yeats's fitful to-ing and fro-ing between Dublin and London continued until 1907, when he moved to New York, where he lived in permanent exile until his death. He could not be persuaded to return. "To leave New York is to leave a huge fair where at any moment I might meet with some huge bit of luck," this Micawber-like prodigal father wrote. "Why do birds migrate? Looking for food—that's why I'm here." Eventually his son worked out an agreement with the wealthy Irish-American lawyer and collector John Quinn whereby the poet sent him manuscripts and first editions and, in return, Quinn helped support the elder Yeats.

Alldritt memorably evokes one of the houses, 58 Eardsley

Crescent in Earl's Court, where the Yeatses lived when the children were still under their parents' roof. In doing so he brings out a strange bit of interaction between nineteenth-century England and America, with the twenty-two-year-old poet stuck in one of the dreariest corners of industrial England pondering a mythic Ireland in his own as-yet-unformed imagination:

An end house in a stuccoed row in the debased classical style typical of mid-Victorian developments, their new home seemed to them even more squalid than the one at Terenure [a suburb of Dublin]. John Yeats himself described it as "old and dirty and dank and noisy," while Lily wrote that the house was "horrible" and the garden just a bit of sooty ground dirtied by cats. Like Terenure, this western edge of Kensington was a lower-middle-class suburb and clearly upsetting to the family of one who had once contemplated practicing at the Dublin Bar. For the large Earl's Court Exhibition ground, which was very close to the house, gave to the area a funfair atmosphere and a noisy vulgarity. Steam organs blared out the music-hall songs of the day and at the time the Yeats family unenthusiastically moved in, Buffalo Bill and his Cowboy and Indian troupe were putting on shows that entailed whooping war cries and rattling gunfire. As the slender, bespectacled Willie went down into the underground station pondering his new project, a poem about Oisin, one of the noble heroes of ancient Ireland, he was met by crowds of working-class cockneys surging up from the steam-hauled trains, eager to cross the street to the Wild West Show.

The precariousness of his upbringing had profound implications for the values he arrived at in maturity. "If I had not been an unsuccessful & struggling man Willie & Jack would not have been so strenuous," John B. Yeats later mused in a letter to a friend; "—& Lily & Lollie? Perhaps they'd have been married like your daughter—a successful father is good for the daughters. For the sons it is another matter."

Yeats's mother comes across as a shadowy non-presence. She seems never to have quite recovered from the shock of marrying a man who proved himself incapable of supporting her in the style to which she was accustomed. In accounts of the Yeats household, she sits silent and resentful in the corner while her husband and her children argue passionately about the Pre-Raphaelites and Irish nationalism. After years of ill health and a series of strokes, she died in 1900, when Yeats was thirty-five. "She was prim and austere, suffered all in silence," Lily Yeats would later remark. "She asked no sympathy and gave none."

It is not difficult to imagine Yeats in this dreary London, dreaming of the country around Sligo he knew as a boy. In "The Trembling of the Veil" from his *Autobiographies* he describes the inception of what remains his best-known poem, "The Lake Isle of Innisfree":

> I had still the ambition, formed in Sligo in my teens, of living in imitation of Thoreau on Innisfree, a little island in Lough Gill, and when walking through Fleet Street very homesick I heard a little tinkle of water and saw a fountain in a shop-window which balanced a little ball upon its jet, and began to remember lake water. From the sudden remembrance came my poem Innisfree, my first lyric with anything in its rhythm of my own music. I had begun to loosen rhythm as an escape from rhetoric and from that emotion of the crowd that rhetoric brings, but I only understood vaguely and occasionally that I must for my special purpose use nothing but the common syntax. A couple of years later I would not have written that first line with its conventional archaism—"Arise and go"—nor the inversion in the last stanza.

Since Yeats speaks of discovering the rhythm of his own music—and unfortunately for the student of meter, he never writes in technical terms about prosody—it might be instructive to scan the last stanza of that much-loved and over-quoted poem (I will use the *accent grave* to indicate secondary stress, partway between the accented and the unaccented syllable):

```
\  *  *  /  *    /  \   *  /  *   /   *   /
I will arise and go now, for always night and day

*  /  /  /  *  /  *   *   /  /    *  *   /
I hear lake water lapping with low sounds by the shore;
```

```
       *    *   /    *    *   /    \   *  \    *   /    *      /
While I stand on the roadway, or on the pavements grey,

  *   /   * *  *    /     /      /
I hear it in the deep heart's core.
```

This is brilliant versification. Yeats usually adapted his verse forms
from his reading, and he may have gleaned this stanza from one
of the nineteenth-century Irish poets writing in English, like
Mangan or Ferguson; its source is unknown to me. The stanza is
made up of three six-beat (hexameter) lines, each divided by a
strong medial caesura. The pause is signaled in lines one and
three by a comma following a secondary stress (\); in line two the
caesura is effected by the unstressed sounds of the second syllable of "lapping" and the unstressed preposition "with." The
fourth line is tetrameter, in accordance with the common principle of rounding off a stanza by moving from a longer to a
shorter line, as in the ballad or the Sapphic stanza. It is all com-
fortably iambic, counterpointed against contrasting rhythms.
The lulling, watery feeling is reflected in several anapestic (* * /)
phrases: "will arise," "by the shore," "while I stand," "in the deep."
The poet's yearning is hammered home with emphatic spondaic
phrases: "low sounds," "deep heart's core."

The metrical approach of other popular lyrics by Yeats in his
Celtic Twilight mode is more conventional but no less beautiful.
"Down by the Salley Gardens" contains fewer metrical surprises:
an inverted trochaic (/ *) foot at the beginning of the first line,
where an iamb would be expected; and the occasional anapest
throughout. A salley is a kind of willow. Here is the well-known
eight-line poem in its entirety:

> Down by the salley gardens my love and I did meet;
> She passed the salley gardens with little snow-white feet.
> She bid me take love easy, as the leaves grow on the tree;
> But I, being young and foolish, with her would not agree.
>
> In a field by the river my love and I did stand,
> And on my leaning shoulder she laid her snow-white hand.
> She bid me take life easy, as the grass grows on the weirs;
> But I was young and foolish, and now am full of tears.

Though the long lines, as printed, contain six beats apiece, each divides naturally into two units of three beats each. The poem reads aloud like a ballad in four stanzas rhyming ABCB, differing from the usual ballad stanza only by virtue of having three beats in the first and third lines of each stanza rather than the usual four. It is utterly lovely and utterly conventional.

As an artist Yeats was restless; he was also proud, and it annoyed him that lesser poets imitated his early work, turning it into an Edwardian period style. Later, well into the new century, he published the following quatrain, titled "To a Poet, Who Would Have Me Praise Certain Bad Poets, Imitators of His and Mine":

> You say, as I have often given tongue
> In praise of what another's said or sung,
> 'Twere politic to do the like by these;
> But was there ever dog that praised his fleas?

As early as 1904, fifteen years after "Down by the Salley Gardens" and eleven years later than "Innisfree," as part of the collection *The Seven Woods* (a reference to the seven woods at Coole, Lady Augusta Gregory's estate), Yeats in "Adam's Curse" hit on the plain-spoken and forceful but still intensely musical form of expression that would evolve into his mature style. Here he abandons the shorter lines and four-line stanzas that typify his early, ballad-like poems for pentameter couplets that owe something to eighteenth-century masters like Swift and Pope. He also—not surprisingly in a man on the verge of turning forty—abandons the languor of his early lyrics for the solid virtues of hard work:

> We sat together at one summer's end,
> That beautiful mild woman, your close friend,
> And you and I, and talked of poetry.
> I said, "A line will take us hours maybe;
> Yet if it does not seem a moment's thought,
> Our stitching and unstitching has been naught.
>
> Better go down upon your marrow-bones
> And scrub a kitchen pavement, or break stones

Like an old pauper, in all kinds of weather;
For to articulate sweet sounds together
Is to work harder than all these, and yet
Be thought an idler by the noisy set
Of bankers, schoolmasters, and clergymen
The martyrs call the world."

Fortunate in many things, Yeats was perhaps most fortunate in the friends he made. Published the year before his death, "The Municipal Gallery Revisited" memorializes several friends, chief among them Lady Gregory, who was for fifty years the poet's patron, confidante, and fellow soldier in the struggle for an Irish theatre, which in itself embodied the struggle to define the emerging nation. In the forceful rhetoric he learned to appreciate from his vacillating father, Yeats—in a rare self-congratulatory mood—celebrates his friendship with Lady Gregory and the third leg of the Abbey Theatre triumvirate, John Millington Synge:

John Synge, I and Augusta Gregory, thought
All that we did, all that we said or sang
Must come from contact with the soil, from that
Contact everything Antaeus-like grew strong.
We three alone in modern times had brought
Everything down to that sole test again,
Dream of the noble and the beggar-man.

The poem continues:

You that would judge me, do not judge alone
This book or that, come to this hallowed place
Where my friends' portraits hang and look thereon;
Ireland's history in their lineaments trace;
Think where man's glory most begins and ends,
And say my glory was I had such friends.

What would have become of the penniless young poet without Lady Gregory, one hates to speculate. From their meeting in 1896 on, she was an ally whose background was reassuringly familiar, in that she was an Irish Protestant, but exotic and exciting in that while Yeats had always been on the outside look-

ing in, Lady Gregory was able to provide him with the aristocratic culture to which he was spiritually attuned. Coole was a
haven where the malnourished young bohemian could be restored to health, with time to write, freed from the pressures of
literary journalism. She became the mother he had never really
had. He reciprocated by turning Coole Park into a symbol for
the ordered, traditional life that represented for him an ideal
organization of culture and society.

Yeats was undeniably an elitist and a snob. The first of these
qualities seems to me, as it informed his views on art and society, a positive value. As to the latter, admirers of his poetry might
be more inclined to regard it as a peccadillo than to recoil from
it in horror. Yeats was prophetic in the alarm with which he
viewed the Roman Catholic nativism that came to dominate the
nationalist movement, culminating in the puritanism and cen-
sorship of Eamon de Valera's Ireland. Yeats had been among
the earliest advocates of Home Rule, but as events moved inex-
orably toward independence he became, like his ally Synge,
more and more an opponent of the merchants and priests who
typified the Catholic Establishment.

In "September 1913" Yeats stirringly elegizes the Fenian John
O'Leary, whom the British sentenced to six years of hard labor
in the stone quarries of the Portland Prison on the south coast
of England, then exiled from Ireland for fourteen years more.
The poem contrasts the idealism of O'Leary, who died in 1907,
to the venality of the emerging Catholic mercantile class which
was coming to dominate Ireland:

> What need you, being come to sense,
> But fumble in a greasy till
> And add the halfpence to the pence
> And prayer to shivering prayer, until
> You have dried the marrow from the bone?
> For men were born to pray and save:
> Romantic Ireland's dead and gone,
> It's with O'Leary in the grave.

R. F. Foster sees Yeats's position as consistent with his spiritual
and aesthetic leanings: "He was clear in his mind that [Catholic

middle-class] institutions represented the faith and assumptions of the majority of the country, and therefore enjoyed a legitimacy not possessed by their predecessors, but he was equally convinced that—for all the rhetoric of nationalist rectitude—they shared many values founded on the debased intellectual currency of Victorian materialism, and its denial of ancient tradition." As for Yeats's increasing love of country-house weekends and dinner parties in fashionable London houses as his fame grew, Foster takes an understanding approach: "Snobbery is never simple, being founded on an insecurity that can be psychological as much as social; and preoccupation with family is a natural response to entering one's late forties childless, with the landmark figures of the last generation crumbling away."

Yeats's elitism was later to elevate eighteenth-century Anglo-Irish culture as an ideal and to focus on the great houses of the aristocracy as symbols not only of beauty but of a distinguished and fully integrated way of life. In making such claims for a class that came—beginning with the land agitation of the late nineteenth century, and increasingly during the Irish War of Independence and the Civil War that followed—to be roundly despised and rejected, many of their houses put to the torch, Yeats was praising a living culture that embodied not what today would be called privilege, but responsibility, wisdom, and dedication. In two great companion poems, "Coole Park, 1929" and "Coole Park and Ballylee, 1931," composed in eight-line stanzas as monolithic and awe-inspiring as marble slabs, Yeats memorializes the life to which he had been introduced by Lady Gregory:

> Sound of a stick upon the floor, a sound
> From somebody that toils from chair to chair;
> Beloved books that famous hands have bound,
> Old marble heads, old pictures everywhere;
> Great rooms where travelled men and children found
> Content or joy; a last inheritor
> Where none has reigned that lacked a name and fame
> Or out of folly into folly came.
>
> ("Coole Park and Ballylee")

Distinguished by an inimitable tone Yeats would call, in "The Fisherman," "as cold and passionate as the dawn," these monumental poems derive some of their power from being prophetic elegies. Yeats knew that the tradition he loved was coming to its end. He bade it, and his friend Augusta Gregory, who in his eyes embodied a tradition of patronage and noblesse oblige, farewell in some of the noblest lines ever written:

> Here, traveller, scholar, poet, take your stand
> When all those rooms and passages are gone,
> When nettles wave upon a shapeless mound
> And saplings root among the broken stone,
> And dedicate—eyes bent upon the ground,
> Back turned upon the brightness of the sun
> And all the sensuality of the shade—
> A moment's memory to that laurelled head.

His prophecy has proved accurate. The house at Coole was pulled down in 1941 and sold to a local farmer for the value of its stones. The lines quoted above are displayed behind plexiglass for the visitor to Coole Park to contemplate.

# A Life in Poetry

Everything I have lived has, usually in some reimagined or sublimated form, gone into my poetry. In what follows I try to tell about those circumstances and events that have formed me as a poet.

We lived in an old house in Memphis that my grandparents bought in 1890. It was a Victorian cottage that was enlarged during the Arts and Crafts period. In the early years of their marriage, South Cox Street was outside the city limits in a little community called Lenox, which had its own station on the L&N railroad line running east from downtown Memphis through what I have called the "whitewashed towns and sparse farms" of West Tennessee. My grandmother's people came from the farming community of Allen's Station, near Brownsville, where the family gathered every year to celebrate Thanksgiving. While the women prepared the feast, the men went out quail hunting through harvested fields where tufts of cotton that had eluded the pickers' hands clung to the ragged plants, and faded corn stalks creaked in the wind. My father shot left-handed and was known as a crack shot. I loved the smell of the spent shotgun shells. One Thanksgiving it snowed, and all of us cousins and aunts and uncles had to bed down overnight in the farmhouse.

My grandfather, Adoniran Judson Williford, farmed near Bartlett, Tennessee, which in earlier days was the county seat of Shelby County. At some point he took up the law and moved to Memphis, where he was active in Democratic Party politics. Eventually he became a judge, and for obscure reasons the people in the neighborhood called him "Squire." In a field next to the

From *Contemporary Authors: Autobiography Series,* ed. Shelly Andrews (Detroit: Gale Research, 1996).

house he grazed his horse, named "Our Bob," after Robert Love Taylor, a popular governor of Tennessee and grandfather of the Memphis novelist Peter Taylor.

A. J. Williford died in the influenza epidemic that swept the country right after the First World War. Because I never had the chance to know him, he became a figure of mystery for me. As a child I used to dress up in his top hat and Chesterfield coat from the attic or poke through his legal papers, which were kept in a big trunk stenciled with the initials AJW. I have his pince-nez and wear his Masonic ring, made of old gold with a reddish tint. The emblem on it is now worn away beyond recognition. He was not a churchgoer. When my grandmother, who was, brought the Baptist preacher to see him on his deathbed—this was during Prohibition—he asked the preacher to go out and find him a bottle of beer. "You're probably the only man in Memphis who could get me one," he said by way of explanation. My grandmother always used to say that I was "a true Williford," by which I think she meant I was proud, had a sense of humor, and was subject to grandiose notions.

My mother graduated from Tennessee College in Murfrees-boro, where she majored in classics. In an old scrapbook I recently found a one-inch item from a *Memphis Commercial Appeal* of the 1920s that reads, "Miss Martha Williford, daughter of Mrs. A. J. Williford, 190 Cox Street, who is a member of the faculty at Snowden School, sailed yesterday from Montreal for Europe. She will visit several countries and will study in Paris, returning about September 1." She remembered this trip fondly and used to tell my brother and me about her little hotel in Paris on the rue Madame next to the Luxembourg Gardens. It's curious to think that Mama was in Paris at the same time Hemingway, Joyce, Stein, and Fitzgerald were flourishing there. For the first few years of my life she taught French and Latin at Miss Hutchinson's, a girls' school near our house in what, as the city has grown and spread out eastward, has come to be known as Midtown. I remember her walking me to kindergarten on her way to her teaching job. The little French I still have, I speak with a Southern accent.

I went to grammar school at Lenox, an imposing brick struc-ture with big granite eagles perched on the cornices overlook-ing its main entrance, four houses down the street from where we lived. Our family took pride in the school because my grandfather was one of the men responsible for its having been built. Lenox School has now been turned into condominiums, but whenever I am in Memphis I visit the school and go round to the spot where my grandfather's name is chiseled into a stone tablet next to the front door.

My father was from Great Barrington, Massachusetts—the descendant of Pardon Elisha Tillinghast, who left East Anglia and settled in Providence, Rhode Island, in 1640. In England the Tillinghasts were Dissenters who went to Cambridge University and wrote contentious books about religion and politics. I found some of their books of sermons in the rare books room in Houghton Library at Harvard. They opposed the monarchy and some of them may have been among the Regicides. Daddy came to Memphis in the early 1930s to work for Proctor & Gamble, met my mother, and lived in the South for the rest of his life. He was an inventor who developed several new machines for the cotton business, including a new cotton compress that he was only partially successful in convincing people in the industry to adopt.

My parents were married in 1932. Many times during my youth I would hear how, the month after they were married, my father's paycheck was reduced by half. Readers of my poems "R.C.T.," "The Knife," and "Father in October" will know him as a straightforward man of integrity. His New England temperament and accent differed greatly from anything else in my experience. My brother David and I thought expressions of Daddy's like "up attic" and "down cellar" were very amusing. America has become so culturally homogeneous now, it's hard to appreciate that in the 1940s a Southerner and a New Englander—my parents, for example—were practically citizens of two different countries. As I grew up, particularly after I got to know New England better, I came to see this mixed cultural heritage as the source of certain conflicts within my own character, and then later, as a strength.

Today it is also hard to appreciate the hold that the Civil War exercised on the imagination of the South as recently as the 1940s. Barry Pickett, a classmate of mine in junior high school, was a descendant of General George Edward Pickett, who led the Confederates' heroic and catastrophic charge at Gettysburg. Fully half of our American history class in junior high school was spent studying "the War of Northern Aggression." While considerable historical reading—as well as insight into the psychological effects of enslavement gleaned from books like Toni Morrison's novel *Beloved*—has brought home to me the evils of slavery, I still regard the Southern struggle as heroic. The threadbare, daredevil troops who followed Lee and Jackson and Forrest into battle won an ineradicable place in Southern hearts. While knowing and accepting most of the reasons I should not love the Confederacy, still, as I wrote in *Sewanee in Ruins*, my long poem about the aftermath of the war in a small Tennessee community,

> my thoughts are with men I have heard of and read of
> who, possessed by a fatal romanticism,
> killed at fourteen,
> ate corn burned in the field,
> and wore the dead enemies' shoes
> in 1865, when everything burned
> but the brick chimneys
> and a way of talking.

I will even confess to getting a lump in my throat when I hear "Dixie." A widely held view of American history has succeeded in defining the Civil War as a contest for or against slavery, but for the white South it was also, and more importantly, a war that tested our ancestors' loyalty, courage, and willingness to fight bravely against impossible odds. That said, I reluctantly no longer have the Confederate flag hanging on the wall of my study, because racists have, sadly, defined it as a symbol of bigotry. A statistic I cited in *Sewanee in Ruins* is that in 1860 only 3 percent of Tennesseans owned slaves. And though my maternal ancestors were among that 3 percent, I still see the Southern cause as a fight to defend the homeland. A story passed down in our family tells of deaf Uncle Joe in Bells, Tennessee, who did not hear the Yankee soldier call out "Halt!" and was shot in the back while riding out of town one day in 1864. I have his watch, a solid gold Elgin with a hunting case.

Shelby Foote, whom I interviewed for the Southern edition of *Ploughshares* that George Garrett and I edited in 1983, summed up the rationale of the average Southern soldier. "This is a rich man's war. You don't have anything to gain from it," a Union soldier called out to a Rebel across the line of battle. "Why are you fighting?" The ragged, hungry Southern veteran unhesitatingly shouted back, "'Cause y'all are down here!" Does this mean I wish the South had won the Civil War? Of course not. I would not like to contemplate what the Confederacy triumphant would have been like. But in the time and place where I grew up, the war lives in memory as the quintessential Lost Cause.

When I was one year and twelve days old the Japanese attacked Pearl Harbor. And though I had not quite turned five when the Second World War ended, I have discovered as an adult what a hold the images and emotions of those years have on me. I stress "images" here. Before I could read, my grandmother—no doubt in an effort to keep me occupied—had me cutting pictures out of the *Saturday Evening Post* and pasting them into scrapbooks. Pictures of fighter planes, aircraft carriers in the South Pacific, the American flag being raised over Iwo Jima—images which were everywhere during the war—implanted themselves in my consciousness. While writing the title poem of my fourth book, *Our Flag Was Still There,* these images, mixed with memories of my own not derived from external sources, came rushing to the surface. Some are seriocomic, like this picture of "Chessie," the Chesapeake & Ohio's advertising mascot, taken from the *Post:*

> One paw bandaged.
> A Congressional Medal of Honor
> red-white-and-blue-ribboned around his neck.
> As convincingly at attention as a military-style,
> family-oriented cat can be in a pullman car.
> On his well-groomed chest, rows of campaign ribbons.
> A dignified, "can do" look
> hovers about his muscled smile.

The generation of men who won the war for us represented authority and security for me as a young child. The affection I feel toward that generation is related to the sense of security I derived from images of our victory in World War II:

> Against a backdrop of blue sky and innocent clouds,
> a line of six blunt-nosed P-47 fighters—
> boxy and powerful like the grey Olds
> we bought after the War
> and drove to the Berkshires for the summer—
> flew off on a mission to Corregidor.

I see in my poetry a continuing involvement with history and politics, as well as a strong inclination to let images carry much of the meaning. Looking back, it seems that I arrived at both of those qualities very early on.

As a boy I spent a lot of time drawing. My perusal of the *World Book,* our family encyclopedia, led me to become knowledgeable about the Napoleonic wars. Like Robert Lowell, the man who would become my writing teacher and most influential mentor when I was in graduate school, I could rattle off the names of Napoleon's generals at an early age. Some of my earliest drawings showed the confrontations at Waterloo between the phalanxes of British infantry and the French cavalry. All through my youth, until I went away to college, I took Saturday, summer, and sometimes evening classes at the Memphis Academy of Art, which in those days was housed in two wonderfully decrepit Victorian mansions in a down-at-the-heels part of town. We learned to draw, paint still lifes, and sketch the models who posed for us in what had been the parlors of an Italianate mansion built by the Lee family, who had made a fortune from Mississippi riverboats. I thought that one day I would be a painter. Though I have not made a career in the visual arts, I can see now how important that training has been to my image-making ability as a writer.

My freshman year at Central High School, playing drums in the marching band looked like a good alternative to being a cadet in our school's Reserve Officers Training Corps. Our band played for weekly military exercises when the cadets marched from Central to their parade ground. My fellow percussionists and I were a mischievous bunch of rebels. We delighted in speeding the beat up to unmarchable levels or substituting for the straight, military 4/4 rhythm an improvised samba beat. The cadets would trip over their brogans and their M-1s trying to keep up with what we were playing, until the order inevitably came for us to bring the beat back to what the sergeant considered acceptable.

My first two jobs were bagging groceries down at the local supermarket and shelving books at the public library. From my earnings at these jobs, my first two purchases were a drum set and a tuxedo. Throughout high school I played in bands: jazz, rock 'n' roll, and country and western. The 1950s were an exciting time to be playing music in Memphis. My brother David played the banjo and I played the guitar, and we learned folk songs from singers in the Ozarks, where we camped and fished and went canoeing in the summers, as well as from the Weavers records and Alan Lomax folk music collections we got from the public library. When we took our instruments to parties for the employees at my father's plant in North Mississippi, there were singers among the black workers who would plug in their amplifiers and play the blues in that Delta style that had been making its way north to Chicago. At country club dances white band leaders like Colie Stoltz would sometimes bring on an old bluesman to play between sets.

Rockabilly was in its prime. Elvis Presley, Roy Orbison, and Carl Perkins were popularizing an eclectic style that brought a rock 'n' roll beat to country-and-western lyrics. Everyone my age listened to Dewey Phillips's "Red Hot and Blue" show on WHBQ, and rhythm and blues was the music we danced to and played in our own bands. The hippest among us listened to jazz; Marvin Stamm, first trumpet in the band at Central High, is now well-known in the world of jazz.

The jazz and rock gigs we played were fairly conventional parties or dances attended by middle-class kids like the ones I went to school with. The country-and-western gigs were something else entirely. I played in a band with three truck drivers, and we were booked into low-life nightclubs, the very existence of which I'm sure my parents were unaware. Memphis has been called the capital of Mississippi; it also acts as a magnet to the surrounding countryside in West Tennessee and across the river in Arkansas. Some of the roughest nightclubs are to be found on the highways that run into town from Millington or Bolivar, Tennessee, or from Mississippi. I remember playing gigs at a dive called the Rodeo Club, halfway out into the county. We would set out for a gig with the piano player driving his old Chrysler, my drums in the trunk, and the bass fiddle filling most of the passenger space—the butt of it resting on the ledge behind the back seat, the fiddlehead resting on the dashboard right under the rearview mirror. The Rodeo Club was famous for its bare-knuckle brawls that would clear the entire club about once every Saturday night. The drum set offered protection when these fights erupted. When somebody broke the neck of a beer bottle on the edge of the bar and went after somebody else, I would get down behind my bass drum and watch the action unfold.

The guitar player would arrive with his whole family in his '48 Buick four-holer. His wife and kids would sit out in the car while we played. The guitar player was really hot, but he drank. At some point during every gig he would pass out while playing. The biggest problem with this was that when he blacked out he would fall backward onto my drum set. Listening carefully to how he played, I would try to anticipate the precipitating moment. When it happened I would leap up and grab him before he hit the cymbals. Then we would carry him out to the Buick, where he would be revived and sent back in to play the next set.

No greater contrast can be imagined than between the Saturday nights I spent at the Rodeo Club and my undergraduate days at the University of the South in Sewanee, Tennessee. As a freshman I was already a reader of such Southern writers as William Faulkner, Robert Penn Warren, and John Crowe Ransom. The sense of the South as a land of mythic dimensions had a strong purchase on my imagination. The small towns of Tennessee, with their white clapboard houses, big shade trees, and memories of guerrilla raids by Nathan Bedford Forrest, took on the dignity of literary distance in Ransom's poems. As I read Warren's *All the King's Men* on the bus during the high school band's tour of Louisiana, the novel's straight slab of highway blended in my mind with the actual road we were traveling. That the real-life setting for William Faulkner's Yoknapatawpha

County was only eighty miles from Memphis encouraged me to believe that I too could make something solid and lasting in words from my life in the same part of the country. Witnessing the transubstantiation of place through the written word has remained for me a thrilling and almost holy experience.

In his memoir, *Lanterns on the Levee*, William Alexander Percy writes of Sewanee—which graduates of the school call "the Mountain"—as Arcadia. It was that and more for me. Dreams of myself as a future artist or musician melted away. Poetry became everything for me; I wrote constantly. The Victorian Gothic fantasy of the college's architecture, the steep limestone cliffs with their views over the surrounding lowlands, the vivid autumns and startling springs—which could begin in February and keep going through May—all of this was like a waking dream for me. I was also caught in the throes of a tragic teenage romance, which in time-honored style contributed to the sweet sorrow of my first year on the Mountain.

Sewanee is an Episcopal college, and in those days chapel was compulsory. My time there predated the recent adulteration of the Book of Common Prayer, so I heard the stately cadences of Cranmer's prayer book along with the King James Bible on a daily basis. An enduring sense of the greatness of the English language seeped into my awareness. Our professors were our idols, however much we might parody them and chafe against their authority. Of all the fortunate things that have happened to me, the experience of studying Shakespeare with Charles T. Harrison, English history with David Underdown, Victorian prose with Abbott Cotton Martin, political science with Arthur Dugan, and modern poetry with Monroe K. Spears was one of my great pieces of luck. Monroe Spears also published a dozen poems of mine in the *Sewanee Review;* these were my first publications.

In the fall term of sophomore year my habits of staying up all night, smoking heavily, and otherwise neglecting my health caught up with me. The doctors diagnosed my hacking cough, which wouldn't go away, as acute bronchitis. Early during Christmas vacation that year I went into the hospital, where about a third of my right lung was removed. When a staphylococcus infection developed in the operation scar, things started to look grave. At the time I drifted in the somnolent euphoria induced by shots of pain-killing drugs, and only later found out that I came close to dying. I actually enjoyed being in the hospital: I listened to music a lot—Gilbert and Sullivan in particular, for some reason—and sketched and wrote. Nowadays I loathe hospitals, but then the place easily replaced the reality of the outside world.

My hospital stay amounted to two months, and then I sat around the house recuperating for some time more. My mother took me to Florida for a while. This experience barely got into my poetry, except in one called "Less Than Yesterday, More Than Tomorrow," which I wrote eight years later while spending a month in Amsterdam. The poem recaptures the convalescent's sense of fragility:

> Rising from sickness
> my bones thin, bending, tender to the touch,
> a lightness in the inner ear
>
> Things seem to rush at me.
> I huddle away from them, my mother driving—
> the street is shocking to the wheels.

The poem, influenced by Sylvia Plath, succeeds pretty well in rendering how strange it felt to leave the hospital, where I floated in a comfortable passivity, feeling very little. The poem closes almost brutally, with the brittle coldness of my adolescent indifference toward my parents:

> Less and less I feel I am falling forward.
> My mother is less patient,
> my father will send me to Florida.
>
> For them I am closing the door to the place
> where the dead children are stored,
> where the pets have gone to Heaven.

From an emotional standpoint, that ending appalls me today. Perhaps my having, in 1966, fallen temporarily under the spell of Sylvia Plath's weird, thrilling, inhumane bravado partially explains my attitude then. Now that I have children of my own, I have a hard time recognizing the young man who could turn such a cold shoulder toward his mother and father, who had gone through the deepest grief during my illness.

Though weakened and subsequently susceptible to colds and bad coughs, I recovered from the operation and infection. Back at Sewanee I was picked to be captain of our College Bowl team. The flight from Chattanooga to New York was the first time I had flown, and I still remember the surge and liftoff as our jet ascended from the airport. New York was a revelation. Just as I had enjoyed the sense of suddenly being taken seriously as an adult with ideas and talent upon arriving at Sewanee, in New York I luxuriated in having left Tennessee behind. Plus, my girlfriend, Nancy Pringle, whom I would later marry, was at Bryn Mawr and could join me for weekends in the Village. Our team did well in the contest, and that meant four free trips to the city. One moment on the quiz show showed me the extent to which I, as the novice intellectual, was still the teenaged rock 'n' roll drummer from Memphis. When asked to give bonny Prince Charlie's other sobriquet (the Young Pretender), I sounded the buzzer and called out, "The Great Pretender"! (For readers who are unfamiliar with rhythm and blues, that's the title of a song by the Drifters.)

When Andrew Lytle came to the Mountain to edit the *Sewanee Review,* he hired me as an editorial assistant during my senior year. Also during my senior year I began to spend time at the nearby Highlander Folk School, where the first stirrings of the civil rights movement were in motion. Folk music became protest music. With a small group of professors and friends, I became gradually aware of the injustices of racial segregation. My attitude toward Southern tradition soured. We had our own, rather genteel demonstrations on the Mountain, and Sewanee was officially integrated. I was suddenly a student radical and couldn't wait to leave the South. I lost the election for editor of the *Sewanee Purple* because of the stand I took against a racial incident on campus. Graduate school at Harvard was the logical next step.

Like the alma mater that she is, Sewanee gives her favorite sons and daughters a high opinion of themselves that is not always justified. Robert Lowell's poetry-writing class at Harvard, which I took side-by-side with my English lit courses, opened me to unfamiliar writing styles and introduced me to some very good poets my age and younger.

Sewanee had one of the best English departments in the country, but it was satisfying to get the graduate education in literature that Harvard's solid, unflashy English department was equipped to give. This meant reading Chaucer line by line in Middle English in B. J. Whiting's class, getting a thorough grounding in eighteenth-century prose in Walter Jackson Bate's course on Dr. Johnson, studying the literature of the English Renaissance with that dry Texan Herschel Baker, who smoked a pipe and delivered his wry observations out of the side of his mouth. Graduate education at Harvard was a revelation of good sense and unhurried reading. Most satisfying to me was the exposure to Old English I got from William Alfred's class. As soon as I heard him read aloud from Beowulf, "The Wanderer," and "The Seafarer," I knew I had stumbled onto a poetry that would remain a touchstone for the rest of my writing life.

My one source of discomfiture was my Southern accent. This was the heyday of Northern awareness of the civil rights movement, and the sound of a white Southern voice was enough to throw one's fellow Harvard students into attack mode. There was a certain irony to this. While most of them had come no closer to the struggle than the nearest television set, I had participated in sit-ins, had confronted the vice-chancellor at Sewanee over his refusal to let Pete Seeger sing on campus, had carried protest signs in Atlanta, had been threatened by rednecks in bars, and had been called names I choose not to repeat. In trying to explain the South to them, it was hard to know where to start.

Meeting Robert Lowell, though, was the experience of my years in Cambridge. Lowell had a genius for friendship. He liked Southerners, and he saw a kind of symmetry in his and my literary migrations. While he as a young New England poet had gone to Tennessee to study with John Crowe Ransom and Allen Tate, I as a young Southern poet had come to Massachusetts to study with him. Lowell had recently published his breakthrough book, *Life Studies*, in which, for most readers, he had left the Paleface stockade by cover of night and joined the Redskins. All true in a sense, but not for those who could appreciate the subtle intermingling of rhyme, meter, and free verse in his new work. While I was learning about free verse from other poets in Cambridge, Lowell was clearly pleased to discover a young poet who could construct a decent stanza. He would read aloud one of my elaborate ten-line stanzas from a poem like "Enter Your Garden" and challenge the other students: "Could you write something that well constructed?" "No, and who gives a damn?" they were likely to say. But the fellow feeling that came from a shared understanding of the craft, as well as some of the familiar Southern ways, bound us together as friends. Through Lowell I renewed my acquaintance with Peter Taylor, whom I had first met at Andrew Lytle's house in Monteagle, Tennessee.

A Lowell poem was not written but built. This was true of his own poems as well as those by writers he admired, like Thomas Hardy, Gerard Manley Hopkins, George Herbert, John Milton, John Crowe Ransom, Elizabeth Bishop. Lowell taught taste, probably without even intending to do so. I define taste—much derided at this particular moment in time—as earned opinion. As the convicts at San Quentin, where I taught in the mid-1970s, liked to put it, "Opinions are like [anal orifices]. Everybody's got one." Taste has a bad name because it is associated with snobbery. But without cultivating taste, an artist cannot grow. Lowell lived and breathed poetry. His attention to the art was thorough and unwavering. Like Elizabeth Bishop's "Sandpiper,"

> His beak is focussed; he is preoccupied,
> looking for something, something, something.
> Poor bird, he is obsessed!

To those of us who were lucky enough to sit around a seminar table or, later, to drink pitchers of vodka martinis with him at the Iruna, near Harvard Square, this single-mindedness was the gift Robert Lowell transmitted.

Working with Lowell was only one of many things that were happening to me during the mid-1960s. In 1964 I became editor-in-chief of *Let's Go: The Harvard Student Travel Guide*. The editorship financed a trip or two to Europe and gave me my start as a travel writer. My parents had sent me to Europe in 1961; just as had happened the first time I went to New York, in Europe I encountered a culture that impressed me as being aligned with the things that were important to me. At least half of the poems in the last section of my first book, *Sleep Watch,* were written in Europe—the genesis of an important circumstance in my writing life. Being on non-native ground, breathing different air, seeing unfamiliar landscapes and buildings, all this gets poems going. Having grown up feeling inwardly alienated from many of the people around me, I came to feel most at home when away from home. I first saw Istanbul in 1964. The exotic atmosphere of the city struck some chord, and I have returned there five times since.

In 1965 I married Nancy Pringle in Charleston, South Carolina. She studied classics at Boston University while I did my graduate work. A Sinclair-Kennedy travel grant from Harvard allowed us to spend the academic year 1966–67 in Europe. We sold the new car my parents had given us as a wedding present and bought a new Volkswagen at the factory in Wolfsburg. The way we handled the grant enabled us to see a lot without feeling we were rushing about like tourists. We spent two or three months at a time in Paris, London, Amsterdam, and Rome, toured Burgundy, Tuscany, the south of Italy, and Greece—including several islands—and made a short trip to Istanbul.

Wherever we stayed we met young Europeans and expatriate Americans. Their way of life, their intellectual and artistic ideas, again broadened my sense of my own possibilities as a writer and gave me confidence to rise above what I considered to be the limitations of American culture. A bohemian culture, the beginnings of what would become "the counterculture" in America, was thriving in Paris and London. We lived in the Hotel Stella on the rue Monsieur-le-Prince in Paris, where, after we had breakfasted on the boulevard St. Michel, I would write poetry during most of the day. Then we would go out to the cafés at night. A friend was studying anthropology at the Sorbonne with Claude Lévi-Strauss—my first exposure to making comparisons between different cultures, a practice that would become part of my thinking from then on. After a psychedelic experience in the apartment of my friend Henry Wolf on New Year's Eve 1966, I wrote my first long poem, "The Old Mill," which took me back mentally to the amusement park at the fairgrounds in Memphis to find a metaphor for the experience. On our way back to the United States, passing through Brussels, Nancy and I bought a copy of a new LP called *Sergeant Pepper's Lonely Hearts Club Band.*

Perhaps during our year in Europe we were exposed to too much that was new. This was the beginning of what has come to be called The Sixties, and its appeal to me was enormous because it seemed to offer liberation in every part of one's life: psychic, sexual, political, literary. Nancy and I separated during the fall of 1967 (to be legally divorced in 1970), and I moved into digs in Kirkland House at Harvard, where I was a tutor. Many of my friends thought I was slightly out of my mind, and they were probably right. But it's hard to tell how much freedom one needs, and at that time I needed all the freedom I could get. The breakup of our marriage wounded us deeply, and the wounds took a long time to heal. The reader of poems like "Come Home and Be Happy," "The Same Bird Again," "Everything Is Going to Be All Right," and "A Letter" from *Sleep Watch* will see how deep the pain went.

Up to that point I had done my course work in the English Renaissance, but now that seemed too—what? Too hidebound, too English, too tradition-bound. I decided to write my dissertation on Robert Lowell's poetry, about which very little criticism had been written at that time. Over the next couple of years I enjoyed going over Lowell's poetry carefully, one line at a time. Later, when I had finished the thesis—in Berkeley in 1969—I never wanted to see it again. But it laid the groundwork for the critical memoir I would write later, *Robert Lowell's Life and Work: Damaged Grandeur.*

I was wild to go to California, where everything seemed to be happening. Academic jobs were plentiful in those days, particularly for someone with a Harvard Ph.D. When the chairman of the Berkeley English department came to Cambridge, I showed up for the interview wearing motorcycle boots and my best suit, which I had had made on Savile Row a few years earlier. As it happened, my interviewer was wearing the same kind of suspenders ("braces," we Anglophiles call them) I was wearing. We had got them at the same shop in the Burlington Arcade. Clearly we had something in common, and soon I found myself with a job offer from Berkeley.

I had never been to California before. I had only the vaguest idea what it even looked like. But I loaded my Volkswagen full of my few possessions and took off for the West Coast. The poet Bob Grenier and his wife, Emily, friends of mine from Harvard, invited me to share a house with them near the UC campus. My years on the faculty at Berkeley are a bit of a blur. I have kept up with only a handful of my colleagues from the English department there: the historical novelist Thomas Flanagan and his wife, Jean; Seamus Heaney, who was at that time a little-known visiting poet; Bob Tracy and his wife, Becky, whom I see in Ireland every summer; and until his death, Tom Parkinson, critic and godfather to the Beats.

The late 1960s and early 1970s were heady days in Berkeley. The campus was the scene of one demonstration after another. Here was the pattern: a campaign of campus demonstrations, followed by police intervention, tear gas, and police charges, with picketing, singing, and rock throwing by the crowd of students, sympathetic faculty, and *lumpen* proletariat from the Berkeley streets. At this point the faculty would decide to go on strike, which meant that you would be manning the barricades with your students, or else the class would be meeting off-campus at your apartment so as not to violate the strike. None of this was particularly good for formal education, but it was exciting and liberating in many ways, I suppose. We learned a lot—though some of what we learned would make our later re-entry into "straight" society difficult.

Part of what we learned was an attunement to wilderness—the environmental movement was in its infancy. My friend Marcia Lawther and I made frequent backpacking trips to the Sierra Nevada, only a few hours away. And in the San Francisco Bay Area you are never far from beaches and parkland. I was also spending a lot of time with friends who were students of a Sufi master from San Francisco; I was gradually becoming involved in the "spiritual" subculture, taking yoga classes, learning to meditate, going for weekends with Tibetan lamas, and so on. My English department colleagues were not thrilled when I proposed to offer an experimental class that would bring some of these practices to the study of works of literature like *Walden,* the poetry of Wordsworth, Allen Ginsberg, and Gary Snyder, and the

Don Juan books of Carlos Castaneda. My chairman decided we would call the course "Literature and Transcendent Experience," which had a respectable ring to it.

Every Thursday afternoon my students and I would drive up to my cabin in Sonoma County and spend two days together reading and discussing books, meditating, doing Sufi dancing, and sleeping out under the redwoods. That cabin near Freestone provides the setting for the first two poems from *The Knife and Other Poems:* "Return" and "The Thief." In memory the place is drenched with an atmosphere of redwood forests and incipient mysticism. I meditated and did yoga for hours on my deck, which overlooked an apple orchard. Suzy Papanikolas, a friend I had met at the Highlander Folk School and traveled with in Europe years before, lived just down the road and taught me Zen.

For three summers in the early 1970s I camped out and taught meditation at the Camp des Aigles, an international school run by the Sufi master Pir Vilayat Inayat Khan in the French Alps near Chamonix, precariously perched on the side of a mountain, with a stunning view across the valley to Mont Blanc. Most of the people who came there were my age or a little younger, and most of them were from France, Britain, the Netherlands, Germany, and the United States. We improvised madly. We turned a shepherd's hut into our kitchen, ran a Honda generator for electricity, slept and meditated in army surplus tents that flooded when it rained. My poem "Legends about Air and Water," from *The Knife,* attempts to capture some of the atmosphere of that mountain retreat.

Pir Vilayat, who taught an eclectic brand of meditation drawn from all the world's spiritual traditions, lectured alternately in English, French, and German. Like most New Age gurus, he slept with his female students, though most of us didn't know that at the time. He also had a wife in Paris and would later have another in California. When I discovered that side of the man I regarded as my spiritual teacher, I felt he had deceived us. Looking back on it, I may have been a bit narrow-minded. I treasure the mad gleam that came into his eyes when in the midst of a spectacular Alpine thunderstorm he would play a mass by Josquin des Prez on his big reel-to-reel tape player—the generator cranking away not quite beyond earshot—and urge us to contemplate the heavenly orders that were so clear to him and so hazy to me. The "spiritual hierarchy"—that invisible government that, in Pir Vilayat's Zoroastrian view of things, fought the everlasting battle of good against evil—had, I now see, some relation to the noble warriors of the Confederacy. If the armies of the masters, saints, and prophets ever need reinforcements on the plain of Armageddon, I'm betting they can count on the astral shades of Generals Lee and Jackson.

In addition to introducing me to the arcane astral worlds that existed perhaps only in his own noble and contradictory mind, Pir Vilayat inspired me to make the pilgrimage to India. On sabbatical leave from the University of California in 1970, after spending most of the summer at the Camp des Aigles, I set out on the overland trip east. This pilgrimage turned out to be even more inspiring, frustrating, comical, and unforgettable than my years under the tutelage of Pir Vilayat.

In 1970 one could travel unhindered overland from Europe to the Indian subcontinent. On the train from Geneva to Istanbul I met an English teacher from Tabriz in Iran who was bringing home boxes of consumer goods, including a television set he had bought in Amsterdam. He taught me some Turkish and Persian phrases, and I kept an eye on his possessions whenever he had to leave the train compartment. I remember the two of us wandering around Sirkeci in Istanbul carrying the TV and the boxes, looking for a cheap hotel, and then having to move from one hotel to another because of the bedbugs.

After putting him and his boxes on an eastbound train a few days later, I went to Konya, headquarters of the Mevlevi dervishes, with a friend from the Camp des Aigles. In Muslim, Hindu, and Buddhist countries the spiritual life of the community centers on some holy place, often a saint's tomb, called a *türbe* in Turkish, around which a shrine has grown up. We spent our first evening in Konya at the *türbe* of Mevlana Celalettin Rumi, a place with a very light, inspiring atmosphere. Mevlana— or Rumi, as he is called outside Turkey—was the founder of the Mevlevi order of dervishes, known for their ecstatic music and dancing. My friend and I happened on the building where the dervish musicians were rehearsing, and sat on the ground underneath the windows for hours listening to them play haunting music on their stringed instruments, hand drums, and wooden flutes.

Inside these shrines rest the massive biers of the leaders of the Mevlevi order, covered in green cloth—green being the sacred color of Islam—with the departed man's massive turban coiled and resting over the head of the long box. Pilgrims walk around the shrine with their palms raised upward in the Muslim prayer posture to receive the blessings of the place. The writings of Pir Vilayat's father, Hazrat Inayat Khan, speak of developing the capacity of attuning oneself to the atmosphere of holy places like the shrine at Konya, and for me this traditional Sufi practice is not that far from the famous sense of place that Southerners are supposed to have. I pay tribute to Mevlana in my poem "Eight Lines by Jalal-ud-Din Rumi," which appears in *The Knife*.

Visiting prerevolutionary Iran, I was taken aback by the hostility I seemed to arouse everywhere I went. Boys in a bazaar once threw stones at me. At first I thought it was because I wore my hair long and sported a big bushy beard, but later I concluded it was because I was a Westerner. The shah was spending millions of dollars celebrating the one thousandth or some other equally fantastic anniversary of the Pahlavi dynasty—a ludicrous exercise, since in reality he owed his throne to American backing, a brutal secret police, and his father, a petty general who had seized power from the democratically elected government with help from the CIA. The country bristled with soldiers. I have never seen such a display of force on the streets of any country in the world. I wanted to visit the meetings of the Kalendar dervishes in Turkestan, but they had been canceled by the government for the duration of the shah's celebration because the Kalendar rites, in which the participants would go into a trance and run metal skewers through their cheeks to prove the power of spirit over flesh, were considered too barbaric for Western eyes.

Who can explain the appeal of travel and of all that is exotic? I was particularly taken with Afghanistan, my next stop east of Iran. This was before the Russian occupation, the war to drive the Russians out, and the civil war that followed, reducing this mountainous home of fierce tribesmen to a wreckage of charred rubble. And long before the Taliban. It seems that every other person walks on crutches in Afghanistan now or is missing an arm or an eye. Twenty-five years ago I saw ancient mosques and adobe forts that dated from the days of the Silk Route caravans and the conquests of the Mongols. I was amazed by Chinese-looking faces out of which peered the bluest of blue eyes—the inheritance of centuries-old racial intermingling. Statues and murals in remote caves spoke of a time when this part of the world had been Buddhist. The history I had imbibed in my own native region went back no more than two hundred years. Here I felt part of historical currents that dated back to wars, migrations, and spiritual and cultural movements that were as old as the human race.

In Herāt, where I spent most of my Afghani days, I bargained for Baluchi rugs in the bazaar and learned pidgin Hindi from other sojourners who had preceded me to India. Then on to Pakistan, where I lived in a Sufi *khankah* and practiced the Islamic rituals surrounding the observance of Ramadan. The sheikh of the *khankah* had a tailor sew me up a suit of the local clothes so that I would not stand out so much in a crowd of Pakistanis. In the Lahore museum I saw art from Bokhara that blended Russian and Central Asian Islamic motifs, once again sharpening my appreciation of the fluidity of cultural traditions in this part of the world. I was overwhelmed by the hospitality of people to whom I had been provided invitations by Pir Vilayat and other fellow travelers on what we called "the spiritual path." Islam fosters a sense of brotherhood unlike anything I have ever experienced.

Eventually, though, I wanted to move on to India, the source of my pilgrimage. War was threatening between Muslims and Hindus on the subcontinent. From the hotel where I had moved at the end of Ramadan I could see crowds demonstrating on the streets of Lahore, calling for confrontation with India. It was in that climate that I crossed the border between the two countries. My first day in India, two things happened: war was declared, and either I lost or someone pinched the pouch that held my passport, my shot record and other travel documents, and eight one-hundred-dollar bills. I arrived in India broke and without any legal identity.

Mysteriously, the pouch turned up in a small town eighty miles from Delhi. Word from the chief of police in the town reached me where I was staying in Delhi, and I took a car there. The chief of police, whose name told me he was a Muslim, invited me to his house, where a good lunch was served on the lawn. Then, as I watched in amazement, he handed over everything from the pouch, including the hundred-dollar bills, whose serial numbers he wrote down on an official form that he asked me to sign. An honest man! I returned to Delhi feeling as if some strange morality play had been acted out for my benefit.

The whole time I spent in India seemed equally marvelous and unreal. With David Freidberg, a friend from California with whom I was traveling at that time, I visited holy men of all persuasions, as well as ashrams, shrines, and temples all over northern India, with results that were sometimes mind-boggling, sometimes laughable. We bathed in and drank water from the Ganges with no apparent ill effects. We roamed the hills above Rishikesh conversing with saddhus, who kept little retreats in the forest. I experienced a startling moment of awakening when we were meditating with an obscure holy man in a small temple in the Himalayan foothills. We were debating some point from the Bhagavad Gita, which I had learned Sanskrit at Berkeley in order to read, when he unexpectedly called out, "Do you understand!?" at the same time striking me on the forehead with his bony, ascetic hand. And then, yes, I did understand.

There is much else to tell about that journey but little room here in which to tell it. Using Kathmandu as a base, I went trekking by myself in Nepal, carrying only a small pack. I would buy food along the way or eat rice and dahl in the little inns to be found along the path in the mountains. In 1970 and 1971 trekking was not as popular and well organized as it would become later. I met other Americans and Europeans occasionally and sometimes hiked with them for a day or two, but mainly I was on my own in a meditative solitude where I was often lonely and introspective, at other times thrilled by views of Annapūrna and the other high peaks above where I was hiking.

As I have suggested, this is a part of the world where out-of-the-ordinary things are likely to happen. I was staying at an inn on the Tatopani River in the Kali Gandhaki Valley in western Nepal when something else happened to me that I still regard with wonderment. Tatopani has hot springs that bubble up in places along its bank, and I was alone, bathing and washing my clothes, recovering from a day during which the trail had climbed two thousand feet and then descended two thousand feet. Sitting in one of the hot springs, writing in my notebook, it suddenly came to me that I would return to America, get married, and have a family. This realization came in a quick series of mental images. I even sketched a little picture of the house we would live in.

Soon my sabbatical time ran out and I was back at Berkeley. To no one's surprise I was not given tenure, and returned to the hippie life most of my friends were living, unhindered by gainful employment. If there is anything to regret about the 1960s (for most of us it began in the mid-1960s and lasted into the late 1970s) it is the excessive emphasis on the nonverbal. In addition to my pursuit of that *ignis fatuus* called "enlightenment," I took up drumming again in the early 1970s and wrote song lyrics. It was possible to draw unemployment and live on my savings for a few years, but eventually it occurred to me that I would have to earn a living. For one who had followed Timothy Leary's advice to "tune in, turn on, and drop out," it came as a hard lesson that, while dropping out was easy, clawing my way back in took every ounce of will, resourcefulness, and determination that I could muster.

Shortly after returning from India, I met and fell in love with Mary Graves. We married in 1973, and our first child, Joshua, was born in 1974. Josh is a professional drummer and bass player, and I attribute his excellent sense of time to his having heard me practicing my drums on a daily basis while he was in the womb. I kept my drum set in our big bedroom in the communal house where Josh was born in Mill Valley. Josh's birth was the most intense experience of our lives to that point. Becoming the father of a son touched off strong feelings about being a man. In "The Knife," which was triggered by Josh's birth, that object, which is not a weapon but a tool, provides a connection between four generations: my brother and me, our father and grandfather, and my firstborn son:

        I see in its steel
            the worn gold on my father's hand
                the light in those trees
        the look on my son's face    a moment old

            like the river          old like rain
        older than anything that dies can be.

   With the pride of parenthood came an impulse to provide for
my family so strong I am tempted to call it an instinct. I have observed it in other young fathers. One of my first jobs was doing
carpentry work for a small outfit; all of us who worked on the job
were musicians. At this time I also maintained and repaired a
succession of Volkswagens, and though it was often frustrating, at
the same time I found physical and mechanical work satisfying. I
had never really worked much with my hands before. This feeling developed into a respect for hard work that I had never felt
before, and I began to work very hard on my poetry. I had a
small workroom above our garage, and I scotch-taped drafts of
poems to the walls. My new book came to life within the four
walls of that room. I was still a hippie, though, and Mary and I
played in a rock/soul music/reggae band called Beauty and the
Backbeats. Playing alongside the bass player Leroy Shyne, I experienced the rock-steady fusion of a tight rhythm section.
   Out of many grease-stained, knuckle-abraded hours spent
solving problems and doing work that my study of English literature had not prepared me for, I earned the long poem "Fossils,
Metal, and the Blue Limit," a somewhat comical meditation on
automobiles, fishing, ecology, and much else. During the days I
spent working on cars I also gained new appreciation for my en-
gineer father and the tradition of inventors and machinists he
came out of. "Fossils, Metal, and the Blue Limit" approaches
that tradition obliquely, from the point of view of the frustrated
amateur mechanic:

        Were days like this foreseen
        in the Platonic heaven of machinists?—
        or by the generations of men,
        with boots and soiled caps and wire-rimmed eyeglasses
        and daughters and sons,

who brought iron ore out of the earth,
learned to smelt it, and formed it into steel?

Eventually, in 1976, I started teaching again. In the college program at San Quentin Prison. If carpentry and automobile mechanics had not been part of my upbringing, the criminal world of my convict students adhered to an altogether different understanding of life. At first prison scared me, with its steel and concrete, its tattooed heavies in their mirrored sunglasses and black watch caps, the armed guards, the gut-freezing clang of the gate that slammed behind me as I entered San Quentin every night. It was the hardest work I have ever done, teaching three-hour classes two or three nights a week. After about six months I became what they called "conwise" and lost the romanticized view of prisoners I had learned in the demonstrations at Berkeley. A lot of the soul and suffering, passion and tragedy, of those men's lives found its way into what may be my best poem, "Lost Cove & The Rose of San Antone," with its lines about this imaginary outlaw, based on the lives of many of my friends from San Quentin:

> The fiddles and autoharp fill up the dark room
> and push out through paint-blackened screens
> into black oaks that press against the house.
> His face hurts me. It doesn't look right.

I felt a bond with these men, some of whom were fellow Southerners, black and white. Some came out of the same counterculture I had been living in. My sympathy for Islam helped me with the Black Muslims, and a shared love for music brought all of us together. At the same time there were evil men there, men whose cruelty and willingness to hurt and victimize could not be explained away by cloudy indictments of that receptacle for all blame, "society."

Our daughter Julia was born in 1979, and finally, six years after leaving the University of California, I was offered a full-time teaching job at Sewanee for a year. Mary, who cried over leaving her friends in California, took to life in Sewanee like a native. She was soon involved in a quilting group there. We lived in a great big stone-and-clapboard house at Morgan's Steep on the edge of a cliff overlooking the valley, and I did research for my long poem *Sewanee in Ruins,* handsomely printed two years later by the university press in Sewanee, with drawings by Ed Carlos, who teaches art at the University of the South. The job was overseen by my friend Arthur Ben Chitty. Andrew Lytle used to talk about the generation of men who had fought for the Confederacy, how they had come home from the war bone-tired and wounded. "Cupid on crutches" was a term much used in those days. The poem explores the 1870s, that defining but often ignored decade when the defeated Confederacy attempted to recover from its losses.

The year 1980 saw the publication of *The Knife and Other Poems,* as well as our move to Cambridge, Massachusetts, where I was offered a three-year Briggs-Copeland lectureship at Harvard. This move reinforced the sense that my career had moved in one enormous circle, starting in Tennessee, moving to New England, then to the West, and now circling back to Harvard again by way of Sewanee. I read Robert Lowell's letters and papers at Houghton Library on a grant from the National Endowment for the Arts, and I finished *Sewanee in Ruins* in the little upstairs office at 34 Kirkland Street, where Seamus Heaney had an office down the hall.

I was once again able to have long conversations with my old friend William Alfred at his house on Athens Street; to drink single-malt Scotch with Stratis Haviaris, who ran the Poetry Room at Lamont Library; to discuss poetry with old friends like Frank Bidart, Gail Mazur, DeWitt Henry, and Lloyd Schwartz; to haunt the Grolier Bookshop, now in the hands of Louisa Solano and her little dog Pumpkin; to carouse with my old friend Peter O'Malley, one of the founders of *Ploughshares,* of which I became an advisory editor. I began doing some reviewing for the *Washington Post.* One day Harvey Shapiro called me from New York and asked me to start reviewing poetry for the *New York Times,* something I did once or twice a year for the next twenty years. I ran a low-budget reading series at Dunster House, where Robert Bly, Stephen Sandy, Derek Mahon, Jayne Anne Phillips, and other writers appeared and read their work for pennies.

I recall fondly two great parties, both held out-of-doors. One was the lamb roast and christening party for Elektra Haviaris. The other was a Derby Day barbecue Mary and I gave at our house in Watertown, when we served barbecued ribs and mint juleps to what seemed like the entire Cambridge literary community. Robert Fitzgerald let me audit his versification class, and I learned from him everything about rhyme and meter that I would later deploy when I returned to that discipline.

After three years at Harvard I was offered a tenured position in Ann Arbor. George Garrett had been hired at the University of Michigan to start up an MFA program, and he brought me on board. This was an offer I was very glad to get. Our sons Andrew and Charles had been born in 1981 and 1983 respectively, and our family of six needed financial security. Charles was two weeks old when we moved to Michigan. Ann Arbor is one of the most liveable small cities in America, one of a handful of communities where one can enjoy the company of other writers and simpatico people in a relaxed atmosphere, hear the best of the world's music, eat at marvelous restaurants, all only a few minutes from home.

We bought a two-story stucco house with four bedrooms, a good fireplace, a porch, and a deck in Burns Park, inhabited by station wagon–driving, softball-playing, PTO-attending, *New York Times*–reading folk, many of whom are my colleagues at the university. After my father died in 1981 and my mother had moved into a nursing home, my brother and I had to sell the house in Memphis. One December morning in 1984 we drove off from 190 South Cox Street in two twenty-four-foot U-Haul trucks, transporting the furniture we had grown up with to our separate homes in Michigan and South Carolina. Our house here has a Victorian feeling to it, and I like sleeping in the bed my parents slept in, using their table silver, hearing, as I write these words, the tick of the Seth Thomas shelf clock from our kitchen in Memphis.

*Our Flag Was Still There*, incorporating *Sewanee in Ruins*, was published in 1984. These new poems concerned themselves with war, with technology, with popular American culture. While preparing the manuscript I formed the intention to write a poem about America during and after World War II, contrasting the generation who fought that war with my own 1960s generation, and I would call it, quoting from the national anthem, "Our Flag Was Still There." This look at postwar America would resemble what I had earlier chronicled about Tennesseans during the aftermath of the Civil War. It was the first time the title of a poem had come first as a concept, and it was certainly the first time I had set out purposely to write a poem that would solidify the theme of the entire book.

In the late 1980s I took a swerve off my path as a poet and wrote a long work of fiction called *Paint It Black*. I wanted to prove to myself that I could write a novel. The book is a thriller, travel book, and love story, with elements of academic satire. The hero is a poet who has to solve a mystery. The agents to whom I showed it thought it would be hard to place, so I gave up on it and returned to poetry. Parts of the book are set in Turkey, and on impulse one summer night in 1987 I decided I would learn Turkish. This spinoff from the project of writing a novel turned out to be endlessly fascinating. Turkish is so hard, so different from English, the mentality so different from our own. I have translated some contemporary Turkish poetry, and in the summer of 1990 I got a fellowship from the American Research Institute in Turkey to take an advanced Turkish conversation class at the University of the Bosphorus. This gave me a chance to reacquaint myself with the city that has intrigued me since I first went there in 1964. And that renewal of acquaintance allowed me to write poems like "Pasha's Daughter, 1914," which was included in my 1995 book, *The Stonecutter's Hand*.

The best thing that has happened to me in the last decade, though, was the year (1990–91) my family and I spent in Ireland thanks to a travel grant from the Amy Lowell Trust. This is a grant given to an American poet every year, the only stipulation being that you live outside America for twelve months. When the Turkish course was over I flew home from Istanbul, and less than twenty-four hours later the six of us took a plane to Ireland, where we had rented a house in Kinvara, a fishing village on Galway Bay. The grant was just enough to live on, and we gladly did without a television, a telephone, and a car. The children went to local schools, and Mary pursued her interest in traditional Irish music and became close friends with the other women her age in Kinvara. I had the great luxury of being able to write every day.

I wrote most of *The Stonecutter's Hand* in Kinvara. I would work at a big table, given me by Jessie Lendennie of Salmon Press in Galway, set before a south-facing window in our bedroom. Or I would hitchhike into Galway and work at a table in Bewley's coffeehouse there or in a snug at one of my favorite pubs: Naughton's, Mick Taylor's, or The Quays. Galway is a medieval city with Georgian overlay. Its streets still follow the curves and digressions of the medieval lanes and alleys. Fragments of old stonework may be seen here and there if you know where to look. Every writer, I suppose, has particularly lucky times in his career when a bit of writing time presents itself just at the moment when he wants passionately to practice his craft. That happened to me in Ireland. "I had my innings there," I wrote in "A Backward Glance at Galway":

> hitching the coast road
> Through salt meadows saturated and green,
> Then walking up from the quays—a wind at my back
> With the North Atlantic behind it, that thinned the coalsmoke
> And refreshed with raindrops the chiseled limestone.
> I would hole up in Naughton's pub with my notebook
> Ferreting words from a secondhand thesaurus,
> Sounding out rhymes in a snug with a pint of Guinness.

Also in Kinvara I started writing literary essays often for the *New Criterion*, the conservative New York monthly, one of the few places in the country that publishes literate, jargon-free essays of ample length and also pays well. Beginning during the year in Ireland, I have written on Rebecca West, William Trevor, Brian Friel, Elizabeth Bowen, W. H. Auden, Somerville & Ross, Bob Dylan, and the Grateful Dead for the *Criterion*, the *Gettysburg Review*, the *Sewanee Review*, the *Michigan Quarterly Review*, and other periodicals. Edmund Wilson is my model for these essays: I like the task of reading deeply and widely into a favorite author and then writing up my sense of that author for like-minded non-specialist readers.

Mary and I spent many nights in Kinvara's pubs listening to traditional Irish music, and it occurred to me that the *Times* might like an article on the experience. They did, and since then I have written often for the travel section—on Georgian architecture in Dublin, driving across Ireland from Dublin to Galway, old churches in Charleston, South Carolina, the Museum of Appalachia in Tennessee, Michigan's wilderness island Isle Royale, Memphis barbecue, and other subjects. This writing combines my love for travel with a way of financing it. In 1995 I published my critical memoir, *Robert Lowell's Life and Work: Damaged Grandeur.* It's a way of paying homage to the poet who taught me much of what I have learned about the art.

**UNDER DISCUSSION**
**David Lehman, General Editor**
**Donald Hall, Founding Editor**

Volumes in the Under Discussion series collect reviews and essays about individual poets. The series is concerned with contemporary American and English poets about whom the consensus has not yet been formed and the final vote has not been taken. Titles in the series include: